Finding Mary

Maynooth Studies in Local History

SERIES EDITOR Michael Potterton

The six volumes in the MSLH series for 2025 demonstrate the enduring vitality of local history as a method and as a lens through which to interrogate Ireland's complex past. This year's studies span more than two centuries – from the late eighteenth to the late twentieth – and traverse the country from Dublin to Donegal, Cork, Limerick, Tipperary and Wicklow. Each book draws on deep archival or oral research to uncover lives, communities and experiences that might otherwise remain obscure.

Angela Byrne's *Finding Mary* reassembles the forgotten story of a 14-year-old Donegal servant girl murdered in 1844. Through a forensic reading of court records, folklore and family testimony, Byrne explores not only a crime, but also memory, silencing and justice in rural west Ulster. The story may be local, but there is an antipodean side to it too. Ciarán McCabe's *The Cork Street Fever Hospital* traces the rise of one of Dublin's most important public health institutions, showing how local and imperial forces shaped its development. In exploring the hospital's work during two major epidemics, McCabe reveals the moral, medical and material dimensions of early nineteenth-century public health in Ireland. David Fleming's *Building Mitchelstown* tells the story of the planned redevelopment of a remarkable Cork town under aristocratic patronage. Yet this is no simple tale of top-down vision: Fleming astutely emphasises the contributions of tradespeople, clergy, investors and others in shaping urban form.

Margaret O'Sullivan's *Lismore Estate under William Rochfort* recovers the complex negotiations between a land agent and tenants across three counties. Using estate papers rich in personal detail, O'Sullivan deftly gives a human face to both landlordism and tenancy in the post-Land War era. Susan Marie Martin's '*Civic evil' and civil disobedience* foregrounds the resistance of Dublin's women street traders in the face of legislation, policing and gentrification from 1882 to 1932. Drawing on police records, council minutes and newspaper accounts, she restores these women's marginal but tenacious presence to the urban historical record. Kieran Devenish's *Factory life* reconstructs the life of a modern industrial workplace – Industrial Yarns Ltd in Bray, Co. Wicklow – through the voices of its former workers. Based on twenty-three oral-history interviews, the study captures a lost world of labour, identity and community in twentieth-century Ireland.

Across all six volumes, we encounter individuals navigating power, poverty, space and memory. Together, they affirm that local history – when rigorously researched and attentively told – offers indispensable insight into how people lived, worked, resisted and remembered. It is a pleasure to thank the authors, the peer-reviewers and the publishers for fastidious work on this year's rich harvest.

Maynooth Studies in Local History: Number 172

Finding Mary: the untold story of an Inishowen murder, 1844

Angela Byrne

FOUR COURTS PRESS

Set in 11.5pt on 13.5pt Bembo by
Carrigboy Typesetting Services for
FOUR COURTS PRESS LTD
7 Malpas Street, Dublin 8, Ireland
www.fourcourtspress.ie
and in North America for
FOUR COURTS PRESS
c/o IPG, 814 N Franklin Street, Chicago, IL 60610

ISBN 978-1-80151-174-2

Printed in England
by CPI Antony Rowe Ltd, Chippenham, Wilts.

Contents

For those whose stories remain untold

Acknowledgments

This book had its origins in a short piece of creative non-fiction I produced (but never published) as part of an online course I took at the Irish Writers' Centre during the first Covid-19 lockdown in spring 2020; thanks to Caelainn Hogan and my fellow course participants for their feedback on my early, tentative attempts at telling this story.

I am grateful to Michael Potterton for accepting my proposal, and for his warm encouragement to pursue this project. Joan Kavanagh generously provided guidance on archives relating to penal transportation; many other historian friends and colleagues gave advice and support, especially Denis Casey and Georgina Laragy; and an anonymous peer-reviewer gave valuable feedback. (Any errors that remain are my own.) Ulster University have kindly provided me with invaluable access to their library and digital resources as an honorary research fellow. My partner, Michael Lavelle, freed me of parental and domestic duties for two weekends of intensive writing in spring 2024, allowing me to immerse myself in Mary Doherty's world and finish the first complete draft of this book.

The staff of the following libraries and archives facilitated my research in their holdings: National Archives of Ireland, National Library of Ireland, Public Record Office of Northern Ireland and the Valuation Office, Dublin. The local librarians in Buncrana and Carndonagh, Co. Donegal, gave of their time and assistance with kindness and generosity.

Most of all I thank the people of Culdaff for sharing their local knowledge, lore and insights. Their words and messages of encouragement and support bolstered my resolve at times when this story seemed too difficult to tell.

Key persons

Mary Doherty, servant, *c.*1830–10 March 1844; places of birth and burial unknown. Survived by at least one brother who had emigrated to America. I refer to her by her first name throughout this book as her name was rarely evoked in the records relating to her murder.

Daniel (Donald) McKeeny, farmer's son, born *c.*1824; convicted and transported in 1845 for sheep-stealing; absconded in 1853, leaving no trace in official records. Throughout this book, I refer to him as 'McKeeny' as this is the most common spelling presented in contemporary sources. Variations of the family name are found throughout primary sources, however, including McKeenny, McKinney, McKinny and McKeeney. I refer to him by his given name, Daniel, even though some official records (e.g., transportation records and newspapers) referred to him as 'Donald'; these forenames were interchangeable at the time.

James McKeeny (*c.*1776–1866), Mary's employer and uncle of Daniel; family details unknown.

Michael Gallagher (*c.*1826–98), a south Donegal farm labourer transported to Australia for stealing cattle on 15 February 1845. He completed his sentence on 12 April 1855 and remained in Van Diemen's Land (Tasmania) as a labourer until his death on 17 October 1898, aged 72.

Mary Gallagher (*c.*1821–72) was granted free passage, together with her sons John (8) and Daniel (6), to join her husband Michael (above) in Van Diemen's Land on 26 April 1850. She died there on 21 February 1872, aged 51.

Timeline of events

1844

10 Mar.	Mary Doherty found dead in Bunagee, Co. Donegal; Daniel McKeeny arrested
15 Mar.	McKeeny taken to Lifford gaol to await trial
28 Mar.	Local residents gather in Loan Fund Office, Culdaff, to give evidence
19 July	Summer assizes, Lifford; McKeeny's trial postponed; Michael Gallagher tried and sentenced to ten years' transportation for stealing two cows
5 Aug.	Michael Gallagher reports McKeeny's 'confession' to the murder of Mary Doherty to the authorities
4 Sept.	Gallagher's report is rejected by the authorities
27 Sept.	Mary Gallagher (unsuccessfully) petitions the lord lieutenant on behalf of her husband, Michael

1845

15 Feb.	Michael Gallagher transported to Van Diemen's Land aboard the *Elizabeth and Henry*
14 Mar.	Spring assizes, Lifford; McKeeny tried and sentenced to fifteen years' transportation for sheep-stealing
19 May	McKeeny transported to Van Diemen's Land aboard the *Ratcliffe*
30 Aug.	McKeeny arrives in Van Diemen's Land

1848

17 Sept.	McKeeny absconds; apprehended 26 September

1850

22 Feb.	McKeeny absconds; apprehended 26 February
26 Apr.	Michael Gallagher successfully petitions for his wife and sons to join him in Van Diemen's Land
30 Aug.	McKeeny absconds; apprehended 3 September

1851

14 Jan.	McKeeny apprehended after absconding on unknown date

1852

30 Mar.	Michael Gallagher granted a conditional pardon

1853

29 June	McKeeny absconds; not apprehended

1855

12 Apr.	Michael Gallagher completes his sentence

Preface

A simple, one-roomed building hides behind a cluster of trees on a Donegal hillside. Easily unnoticed by passers-by or dismissed as another neglected byre. Somewhere to store fodder or long-forgotten and rusted implements. Nothing to see. Nothing remarkable can ever have happened in this place of spit and calloused hands, of hardscrabble existence.

In March 1844, 14-year-old Mary Doherty was bludgeoned to death on this very spot. The crime rocked Inishowen and made national and international news.

Since leaving London to return to Ireland's north-west in 2015, I've trawled folklore, old newspapers and histories for past tragedies that may have given my Culdaff ancestors cause for grief or fuel for gossip: murders, drownings, accidental deaths. Some intrigue me, like the bog body disturbed by turf-cutters from its rest under an eight-feet thick blanket of peat and moss in the townland of Muff, or the poor woman who died in agony at the age of 46, said to have accidentally taken carbolic acid, thinking the bottle contained whiskey. But it's my neighbour, Mary, who haunts the ancient sheep trails that weave through thick glossy rushes and gleaming yellow whins, where surely her long skirts once snagged.

I visit Mary on the anniversary of her death.

The place sits on a narrow country road leading from Culdaff village to Carthage Mountain. The road is steep and dotted on each side with neat, nondescript bungalows in creams and yellows, their too-large eyes blank and gaping. The thick, unruly hedgerows, potent with the promise of the coming summer, are interrupted by painted and capped boundary walls. Moulded cement pillars and garden ornaments totter absurdly on naked lawns. The stretch is silent except for my own breath and the rasp of my boot soles on gravel.

Set back off the road, the cottage peers through a bare, wind-whipped wreath of gnarled ash and sycamore. It's the only one remaining of the cluster of low, stone buildings that used to huddle here. A dry-stone wall crouches at their feet, daubed with blooms of white lichen. It is purposeless, remaindered, holding fast to a boundary that exists only in the stones' insistence on remaining arranged one on top of the other. The trees lean in protectively towards the cottage, casting shadows over the flat of the former farmyard, its lush green painted from the leavings of long-dead pigs, chicken and cattle. The glittering bay is just visible to the east. A wedge of swans honks its way from the estuary and up overhead. At this elevation, the morning sky is like an upturned bowl, vaulted and tinged with the last hint of winter's white light.

Birds chirp in the hedgerow as I cross the small, waterlogged field, making my way between the clumps of bottle-green rushes with their dry, burnt tips. Earthsmell rises as my boots sink into the soft ground. I follow the barely distinguishable rut of the path to the cottage, overgrown with disuse. A few tumbledown stones mark the gentle curve towards the snug bower.

Short, lime-green grass carpets the once mud-caked farmyard. A robin hops, businesslike, across my path. An ancient lime render clings to the cottage walls, a mottled neglect. Someone has replaced the thatch with a corrugated iron roof. It gleams oddly, the signal of a shift, one of the countless buildings that went from being loved to being used, their families long departed to distant shores or to more modern bungalows. The weathered metal warns ramblers and amateur photographers to keep their distance, the building might be in use, the farmer might be just around the corner. It's also a lid on the cottage's dark secret, and the terrible events that few remember.

Culdaff,
March 2024

Introduction

This is a true story.

But it is also a story that insists we think carefully about who gets to do the telling.

Julia Laite, *The disappearance of Lydia Harvey*, p. x.

On 27 September 1844 south Donegal woman Mary Gallagher made an appeal to Baron Heytesbury, lord lieutenant of Ireland. Her husband, Michael, had been sentenced on 19 July to ten years' transportation for stealing two cows. Her one-page letter (likely dictated by her to another person), composed in a single run-on sentence, breathlessly pleaded her husband's 'peaceable character' and previously clean record (fig. 1). Her entreaty closed by outlining the family's circumstances: Mary was left with two small children to feed, the younger just three months of age.

She may not have been exaggerating in describing herself as 'most miserable and distressed'. The prospects were bleak for any woman abandoned, widowed or otherwise separated from her spouse. The means by which women in Donegal could earn money were limited – domestic service, spinning and knitting were the most common (see table 1) – and it is unlikely that Mary could have supported the household.[1] Women were much more likely than men to be destitute, as recorded by a parliamentary enquiry into poverty in Ireland in 1835–6.[2] In the decades preceding the Great Famine emigration was on the rise, but the array of assisted emigration schemes that would emerge after 1846 were not yet available to Mary and her small children.

On 4 September the authorities made their decision that her husband's sentence of transportation 'may be carried into effect without further delay'.[3] With the dreaded workhouse beckoning – the one in Ballyshannon had received its first inmates in May 1843 – the despairing woman made a plan for survival, leveraging a recent

To His Excellency Lord Hestesbury
Lord Lieutenant General Governor of Ireland
The Humble Petition of Mary Gallagher
Most Humbly Sheweth

That your Excellency's Petitioners Husband Michael Gallagher is now Confined in Lifford Gaol in the County of Donegal for Cow Stealing Since last Assizes that the prison=er is under Sentence for Transportation and from his Childhood till the present unfortunate crime took place for which the prisoner is under sentence for, never before this case the undersigned can Certify that he had never been accused or impeached for break=ing the public peace and that he always maintained a peaceable honest character, That your Petitioner has became most miserable and distressed having two small Children the youngest of whom are only three months old, and has no probable means of Support since the fate of her unfortunate Husband therefore Petitioner most humbly and respectfully im-plores the Compassion of your Excellency and be pleased to take poor Suppliants Case into Consideration and mitigate prisoners sentence of Transportation to imprisonment, And Petitioner will ever pray

I Believe the above statement to be true ...

27th September

1. Petition of Mary Gallagher to the lord lieutenant of Ireland, 27 September 1844 (National Archives, CRF/1844/G26: https://nla.gov.au/nla.obj-2293652468/view; courtesy of Director of the National Archives).

murder in the farthest part of the county in a desperate attempt to have her husband freed.

This book explores the background to Michael and Mary Gallagher's plot to secure his freedom: the murder of 14-year-old Mary Doherty in the rural townland of Bunagee, Inishowen, in 1844. My purpose is not to cast guilt on any party, but to fathom Mary's world, and the worlds of those around her. However uncomfortable it may be, this is also the story of her murderer, his family and those who tried to use her brutal death to their own ends. Her murder, and the subsequent investigation and trials, provide insights into the lives of those involved, the society in which they lived and their relationships with the structures of the state. These humble people left behind few records in their own words; Mary Gallagher's letter to the lord lieutenant, who would have dealt with her petition personally,[4] is a valuable rare example of personal testimony from a woman of her station in the period. This book is an attempt to reconstruct the experiences and understand the actions of those enmeshed in the murder of a child in pre-Famine rural Donegal – a world in which community was everything, and inter-personal relationships the foundation upon which entire lives were built.

This book might be referred to as a microhistory – what historian John Brewer describes as the study of 'a remarkable event that enable[s] us to open up an otherwise obscure social world'.[5] At the heart of this endeavour, in Brewer's words, 'is a commitment to a humanist agenda which places human agency and historical meaning in the realm of day-to-day transactions and which sees social reality as grounded in the quotidian'.[6] While microhistory emerged in the 1970s with strong representation from historians of France and Italy in particular, Irish historians were slow to embrace the approach. Angela Bourke's masterful *The burning of Bridget Cleary* (1999) remains, arguably, the most notable Irish contribution to the genre, while Breandán Mac Suibhne's *The end of outrage* (2017) is a recent important addition to the literature. That said, local studies has long thrived in Ireland, not least thanks to the dedication of local history societies across the island; the individual efforts of scholars like the late Raymond Gillespie, who established the Maynooth Studies in Local History series and oversaw the publication of 150-or-so volumes under that imprint; and long-standing respected projects and series publications such as the Irish Historic Towns Atlas and Geography Publications' county histories series.

My own approach is informed by a background in cultural history coupled with a deep awareness of the imprint of local folklore and storytelling. As a child, I was taught stories embedded in the landscapes of the town in which I grew up, the glen in which my father spent his childhood and where we visited most weekends, and the townland of Bunagee, where my paternal grandmother was born and where I have spent long periods of time. Individual fields, even significant rocks, had names and stories attached to them; each place-name decoded a story that had its place in the wider narrative of Irish history over the longue durée. Historian David Fleming reflected on the study of everyday life – an important element in microhistory – within Irish historical studies more widely:

> Historians have a tendency to focus on the extraordinary at the expense of the mundane. As a result the portrayal of the past is sometimes skewed in favour of events that bucked the normal trend or individuals who appeared to alter the course of things. The humdrum may be scorned as less interesting, harder to document, and of little or no consequence. But to see it as trivial or unimportant is to betray the past and the varied lives that individuals led. The study of daily life is important, if only to provide a context for understanding the events and flashpoints that form the overarching narrative of our histories.[7]

In 1972 the late Donegal local historian Brian Bonner wrote:

> Too little attention has been given to the life of the ordinary people. […] The throbbing pulse and beating heart of the nation are found among the people who are concerned with the basics of living and surviving. These are in general the poor, the unknown and the downtrodden. Anyone interested in the story of Ireland will note with dissatisfaction that practically nothing is known regarding the day-to-day life of past generations. This lacuna is a permanent hurdle to a full understanding of the real effect of national events.[8]

Bonner was calling for a telling of history that has since, in Joan Scott's words, 'grant[ed] agency to those who have heretofore been "hidden from history" or left on its margins'.[9] I hope that he would be pleased to see the flourishing in local history across Ireland since then, and that he would welcome this small contribution to the study of Inishowen history.

Part of what this book demonstrates is the interconnectedness of the life of the 'ordinary' person and the wider world. Big themes like emigration and empire emerge in understanding why Daniel McKeeny burgled the house in which Mary Doherty worked, while local and community approaches to disputes are illuminated through the protracted process by which McKeeny was finally convicted, albeit not for Mary's murder but for sheep-stealing. So, uncovering the details of a largely forgotten murder contributes to historical understanding of the ways in which global systems impacted on the lives of individuals who appear far removed from centres of power.

More than that, this book gives voice to people who might be considered voiceless, none more so than Mary herself, a child murder victim whose name was recorded only four times in the historical record.[10] This book pieces together scraps of information from an array of sources: contemporary newspapers (where I first came across this story), Irish, American and Australian civil and church registration records, maps and surveys, Irish legal records, Australian transportation archives, and oral histories – what Julia Laite has described as 'a large number of very small details'.[11] Throughout, I have attempted as carefully as possible to interlace those fragments into the broader narrative of Irish and global, imperial history to illuminate the lives of, and worlds inhabited by, this story's main characters.

This is where the personal background of the historian comes in, as it so often does in the writing of microhistory and local history. I have direct ancestral links to Bunagee going back to at least the 1820s. One of those ancestors was a bachelor granduncle who lived most of his life in Bunagee, and who lived in my childhood home during his later years. He recounted local lore and told us many stories about his life as a fisherman, but he never once mentioned the historic murder of a child that happened within a few hundred metres of his lifelong home. I cannot ask him now whether his parents had ever told him the story; whether it had been passed down from his great-grandfather, William Monagle, who may have been one of those gathered in the Loan Fund Office in Culdaff in April 1844 to provide witness statements, or hear the statements given by others.

Despite the silences, the forgetting, and the gaps in the documentary record, the story of Mary Doherty's murder has survived in local lore. I am grateful to members of the local community who generously shared the versions of the story they heard from their own forebears. The factual inaccuracies and embellishments that emerge from the oral tradition reveal something of the Ireland that came later – post-Famine and post-Independence – and in the closing chapter I offer the socio-economic circumstances of those days as partial explanation for the ways in which Mary's violent death has been remembered and mis-remembered. Now that this historian has pieced together local lore, official records, first-hand accounts, newspaper reports and other sources, I hope that a dark chapter in our local history can be understood in new terms, and received as a window into lives that are in some ways so very far removed from what is familiar to us today but, in many others, innately recognizable for the central role of community and community relationships.

1. Life in Culdaff in 1844

> I love my country and respect its [distilling] laws; but I could not at that moment subdue the wish that these poor people were beneath its cognizance; for (God help them!) they had need have something to keep them warm and in heart amidst these rugged mountains.
>
> Anon., *Notes of a journey in the north of Ireland in the summer of 1827* (1828), p. 16.

The mountainous Inishowen townlands of Bunagee and Carthage (formerly Ballycarrow or Ballycarron) sit on the northern edge of Culdaff village, bounded to the north and east by the Atlantic and to the south and west by mountain and bog. Culdaff is set along a single street along the main routeway that cuts across the narrow northernmost extremity of Inishowen – a peninsula on a peninsula.

In the early 1840s Culdaff village was small but thriving. Nestled within a meander of the Culdaff River, the south-eastern end of the village tapers out into a Y, diverging at the small village green (fig. 2). This was for generations the heart of the village and of the wider rural parish, home to the Loan Fund Office (a public gathering place, as we shall see later), a dispensary, a forge (where men traditionally congregated to share news), and the Church of Ireland church. The fair green – host to quarterly fair days, occasions for trade and socializing – lay behind the Loan Fund Office. The small, early modern burial ground of Ardmore sat on the slight rise behind the forge, to the south-east of the village green; it fell into disuse and Catholic burials moved to the graveyards at Bocan and Aughaclay churches, probably from the early 1830s onwards. The village boasted a police barrack, a parish school for boys and a second school supported by the landlord, George Young (1792–1877). Some handsome two-storey townhouses and commercial premises had been erected along the main street in the previous twenty years, designed with the refined, plain regularity

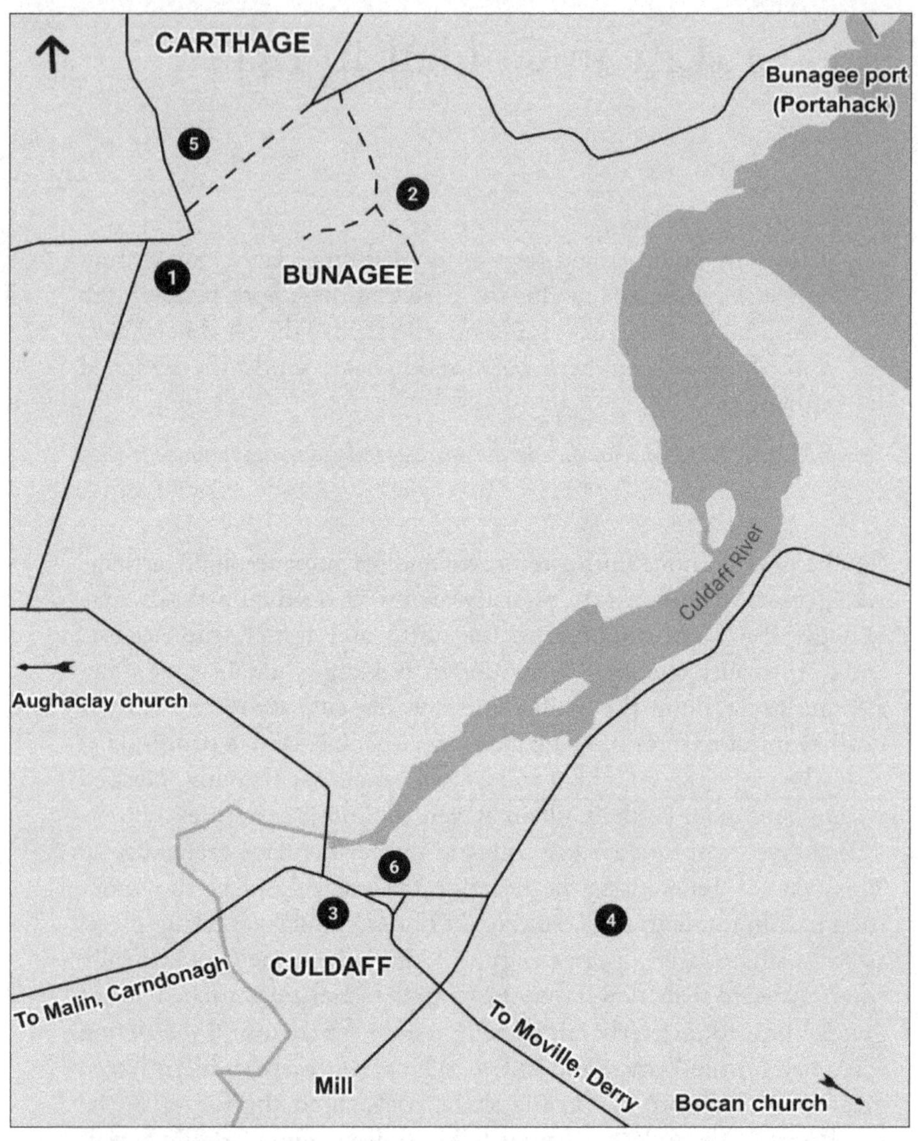

2. Map of Culdaff and Bunagee, *c.*1840, showing places mentioned in the text. Key: 1. House of James McKeeny and Mary Doherty's place of death; 2. Cluster of McKeeny family plots; 3. Police barrack; 4. Culdaff House; 5. Carthage House; 6. Loan Fund Office.

characteristic of the age. Still, sited a few miles (9km) north of the market town of Carndonagh, but eight hours' walk over mountain and coastal road from the port city of Derry, the place was almost unimaginably remote before the advent of railway, bicycle or motor car.

Today, the name Bunagee is understood as referring to the narrow strip of low-lying land between the foot of Carthage Mountain and the Culdaff River estuary. Its focal point is Bunagee Pier and the surrounding suite of coastguard buildings constructed *c.*1870: a lifeboat station and coastguard cottages. In 1844, however, and up to the early twentieth century, the place-name Bunagee (or Bunnagee) designated a scattering of dwellings and small farms on the hillside a little to the west of the port, immediately to the north of the present-day Bunagee Road, which was laid out in 1841.[1] The townland of Carthage is now commonly understood to refer to the hillside overlooking the estuary and pier. It is still known in Irish as *Bun an Ghaoith* (anglicized as Bunagee), however, denoting 'the bottom of the river-mouth'.[2] In 1830 John O'Donovan recorded two Irish place-names in the area – *Baile Cairn* and *Bun na Gaoithe* – and two English names: Cartage or Carthage and Bunagee. The name 'Carthage' may have been imposed on the area when Carthage House was built in *c.*1775, although 'Calridge' was recorded in 1776, and the present name may be a corruption of this earlier form.[3]

Life in Culdaff parish was overwhelmingly rural and time was marked by the seasons, the major feast-days and fairs, and the agricultural calendar: lambing, ploughing, seasonal migration, saving the turf, harvest, herring fishing. In 1841 Culdaff village was home to only 133 people, but the parish had 5,750 inhabitants.[4] Some minor industries tried to capitalize on the raw materials available locally: limestone and flagstone were quarried for export, a tuck mill ran on the Culdaff River, and a corn mill operated since the 1780s, when the milling industry began to flourish across Ireland.[5] Indeed, Samuel Lewis's *Topographical dictionary* recorded in 1837 that Culdaff village was popularly known as 'Milltown', and an 1814 map of the area named the village as such.[6] Culdaff River and Bay were sources of salmon and cod, and the extensive sand dunes were home to rabbit warrens.[7] A majority of families depended on agricultural labour (see table 1) but, in 1837, it was estimated that only a third of the land in the area was suitable for cultivation.[8] The townland of Carthage, measuring over 1,497 acres, had a total valuation of £353 5*s.* in 1857; of its 101 households, 44 per cent were living on holdings valued at

£2 19*s*. 19*d*. or less, and 18 per cent on holdings valued at 19*s*. 19*d*. or less. The best land sat within the demesnes of the surrounding 'big houses': Culdaff House, Malin Hall and (to a lesser extent) Carthage House.

Table 1. Occupations declared by more than 1,000 people in Co. Donegal, 1841. Adapted from *Census* 1841. This table clearly shows the importance of women's paid labour in the rural economy, with female spinners outnumbering servants and labourers of both sexes

Occupation	Male	Male U-15	Female	Female U-15	Total
Spinners (all kinds)	1	-	39,840	2,380	42,221
Servants & labourers	37,026	4,181	490	89	41,786
Farmers	26,181	1	468	-	26,650
Servants (domestic)	920	178	4,224	501	5,823
Knitters	-	-	3,144	515	3,659
Weavers (all kinds)	3,275	13	82	4	3,374
Herds	281	1,589	117	636	2,623
Paupers	265	183	1,009	221	1,678
Boot & shoemakers	1,590	25	15	-	1,630
Dressmakers	-	-	1,090	25	1,115
Tailors	1,024	32	1	-	1,057

3. Culdaff House, 1899 (courtesy of National Library of Ireland).

4. Carthage House (courtesy of Alistair Rowan/Buildings of Ireland, Irish Architectural Archive).

Culdaff House, built by George Young the elder (1715–82) in 1779, was located at the eastern end of Culdaff village (fig. 3). Set well back from the road among deciduous trees, the well-proportioned house, handsome landscaped grounds, walled garden and summerhouse were contained behind stone walls interrupted by snug gate lodges. The first-edition Ordnance Survey map (1834) depicts well laid-out woodlands and formally planted gardens with fashionable serpentine pathways.[9] The Young family had been in Inishowen since the mid-seventeenth century, rising in prominence with each generation. George Young junior (1792–1877) was what was referred to as an 'improving landlord' with fine farmland on his estate and an active interest in promoting more modern approaches to cultivation. By 1856 his holdings peaked. He had amassed an estate of 10,500 acres (4,250 hectares) with an annual income of over £3,000 – but soon lost the greater part of it through lavish living.[10]

John Harvey (1802–68) inherited Malin Hall on his father's death in 1820 and became high sheriff in 1836.[11] His paternal grandmother was Elizabeth Young, daughter of Robert Young of Culdaff House; the families were closely connected. Malin Hall, built *c.*1758 and sited to the west of the picturesque village of Malin, was described by a contemporary as 'a well-wooded demesne, which forms a great ornament in this bleak neighbourhood'.[12] Harvey was said locally to have planted several thousand trees on the demesne in the first decade of the nineteenth century.[13] He experienced resistance in the early 1830s when he enforced the collection of the tithe, requesting in winter 1833 that the police force in Inishowen be increased following his receipt of a threatening letter.[14]

Carthage House, a mile (1.6km) north of Culdaff village, was built in the 1770s (fig. 4). In 1844 it was home to Revd James Knox, who had been headmaster of Derry Diocesan School from 1794 until 1834, when he retired to Carthage.[15] The first-edition Ordnance Survey map shows the grounds of Carthage House – more modest than the extensive parklands at Malin Hall and Culdaff House – with their surrounding rubble walls, long, formal entrance and planted woodland. The five-bay two-storey structure designed in a pared-back Classical style must have seemed impossibly out of place next to the townland's 100 other households, mostly modest one- or two-roomed thatched stone houses. In 1857 *Griffith's valuation* assigned an annual value of £4 10*s*. to the house and the nine acres (3.6 hectares) on which it stood; no princely sum. By contrast, Culdaff House was valued at £130. Still, Carthage House and grounds were respectable enough to be described in 1837 as being among a minority in the area that were employing 'an improved practical system of agriculture'.[16]

The residents of the 'big houses' enjoyed a life very different to the majority of their neighbours. Their relationship with their neighbours was defined by the payment of rents and this was the main matter that brought landlords into direct contact with the tenantry.[17] George Young kept a diary that is detailed enough to paint a complete picture of life at the provincial 'big house': daily walks along the shore, regular inspections of the village mill and tenants' farms, annual visits to the spa at Cheltenham to treat a stomach complaint, and regular visits to Derry on legal and administrative business. In the summer, visitors would come to Culdaff to bathe, enlivening society for a time, and on 12 August every year Young hosted his tenants for a party in honour of his own birthday: a tea party for the schoolchildren and a dinner in the barn for the labourers.[18] Young's son, Robert (1834–1912), had an idyllic childhood, bathing regularly in Culdaff Bay, raising rabbits in the grounds of Culdaff House, and receiving lavish and expensive gifts on his father's return from trips to England.[19]

In 1835 religious ministers serving the parishes of Culdaff and neighbouring Clonca reported on the material conditions of living in the area. Revd John Canning stated that most houses were built of stone with earthen floors, and most families' possessions consisted of

> a small chest, a few rough stools, and a small table, a pot, a few noggins, a wooden spoon, a few plates, and a few iron spoons [...] one bedstead, formed of sticks, and one or two beds on the ground; the bedding is generally of a very bad description.[20] (The bedding was often straw scattered on the floor, or plaited to form a mat.)

Canning's testimony is only marginally less grim than a description furnished in 1814:

> The cottages are in general extremely deficient in point of cleanliness: as they seldom have a chimney, they are almost always full of smoke. Large heaps of filth lie across the doors; and in some instances cows and horses are inmates with the family. [...] hence it follows that, notwithstanding their hardy constitutions, they are subject to diseases which frequently cause extensive mortality.[21]

An anonymous woman visiting Inishowen described the exteriors of both cabins and larger farmhouses as consisting of '[a] stack of turf, a stagnant pool, and an offensive heap of refuse'.[22] She also described clusters of hovels where 'unhosed and unshod, [the people] scramble through life'.[23]

5. Typical rope-thatched dwelling, near Culdaff, Co. Donegal (courtesy of National Museums Northern Ireland/Mary Evans).

Accounts of the standard of living among labourers and tenant farmers must be treated with care, as many observers wished to emphasize an exotic poverty – yet, the vast majority of homes were small and simple, uncluttered by possessions but often crowded with people (fig. 5).[24] The cast-iron pot for boiling potatoes was ubiquitous, and essential.[25] Many of the tools and implements used around the house and in farming were crafted from cheap or free, readily available sources. Willow ('sally rods') was woven to form lobster pots or shallow baskets that served as potato-strainers and communal platters; pitchers, noggins and drinking vessels were crafted from wood; straw and hay was plaited into hardwearing horse collars, or woven to make mats for sleeping.[26] Inishowen memoirist Charles McGlinchey (1861–1954) recalled that in the 1860s/1870s, people owned only what they could manufacture themselves, and that all utensils were made of wood; every home owned six or seven noggins and pigins for carrying, storing and serving liquids.[27] Local Culdaff lore collected from an informant born in the 1880s recorded that those who could not afford candles would light their homes with bog-deal (narrow lengths of dried bog wood).[28] The standard of living is corroborated by the census of 1841, which recorded that of Culdaff parish's 984 inhabited houses, 523 were deemed 'third class', meaning they had windows and two-to-four rooms; and 243 were 'fourth class', that is, one-roomed mud cabins where families – often three generations – ate, slept, argued and played in the dim turf smoke.

An informant in 1814 described the standard diet in the parish of Culdaff: potatoes, oatmeal porridge, eggs, milk, butter, fish and tea; 'butcher's meat is seldom used'.[29] A contemporary in nearby Clonmany grumbled: 'The beggars flock from other districts to this, as it abounds with potatoes, which are the chief aliment of the poor in times of scarcity, so that they are sometimes very troublesome to us' – so much so, that in the previous year the parish decided to refuse alms to all except the 'lame, the decrepid [*sic*] and the blind'.[30] The same writer noted the harvesting of shellfish and seaweed for consumption in times of scarcity.[31] The unnamed female visitor to Inishowen in 1827 found four 'very ill-clothed' children in a cabin in south Inishowen 'devouring oysters fresh from the Swilly', which the woman of the house shared readily with her visitor (an indication not of sufficiency, perhaps, but of hospitality and pride).[32] Clonmany native McGlinchey described the typical diet of his childhood in the 1860s as consisting of milk, fish, soups of seaweed and shellfish, boxty, eggs, corn bread baked from home-ground meal and spread with home-churned butter, and sowens for supper, sometimes mixed with carrageen; tea was not taken in the area at that time.[33] The historian approaches sources like travellers' accounts with a degree of scepticism, prone as they were to exaggeration and hyperbole, but the consistent emphasis on poverty and subsistence living indicates widespread hardship alleviated only by the ingenuity, effort and hard work of all members of a labouring household, down to the youngest child. Families expended their time and energy on their own crops of potatoes and oats, and on rearing poultry and pigs, to support themselves. They sold turf, oats, eggs and poultry, and products like yarn to pay their rent and bills for tobacco, salt, other goods they could not produce themselves, and the services of the priest for baptisms, funerals and 'churching' of women after birth.

There was one dispensary for the parish of Culdaff, established in 1817 'for the relief of the poor inhabitants' of the parishes of Culdaff and Clonca. The principal diseases for which an average of 1,800–2,000 people were treated annually were fever, rheumatism, heart conditions, dyspepsia, 'female complaints', fractures and dislocations. A House of Commons report of 1835 advised that 'particularly in the poorer districts of the country where disease much abounds [...] much more good might be done' by an increase in funding to the dispensary.[34] Inishowen Poor-Law Union was established in 1840. One of Co. Donegal's eight workhouses and serving Inishowen district, Carndonagh workhouse opened in October 1843 with accommodation for 600.[35]

Table 2. Religious denominations in Culdaff parish, 1861

Culdaff parish (rural)			
Denomination	**Male**	**Female**	**Total**
Church of Ireland	181	158	339
Roman Catholic	2,098	2,146	4,244
Presbyterian	95	77	172
Methodist	20	20	40
Total (rural)	*2,394*	*2,401*	*4,795*
Culdaff town			
Church of Ireland	23	24	47
Roman Catholic	24	23	47
Presbyterian	1	5	6
Methodist	0	0	0
Total (town)	*48*	*52*	*100*
Overall total			**4,895**

Source: *Census* 1861.

The religious needs of the people of Culdaff were served by both the Established and newly emancipated Catholic Church. The mid-eighteenth-century St Boden's Church of Ireland church, located in the heart of the village, was extended in 1828, and new places of worship emerged to serve the newly invigorated Catholic faith from around 1830. An existing church at Aughaclay (Templemoyle), around 3km from the village, was rebuilt on a larger plan in around 1830, while another new church dedicated to St Mary, lying 1.7km to the south of Culdaff at Bocan, was built in 1824.[36] In the absence of earlier statistics, the 1861 census indicates that the religious profile of the parish was overwhelmingly Catholic (see table 2). But, in 1844, the post-Famine stranglehold of the Catholic church on social, political and family life was not yet an imaginable prospect. Folk traditions were carried on vigorously in tandem with formal worship. The local pattern at Turas Boden (St Boden's Well) on the bank of the Culdaff River, just behind the Church of Ireland graveyard, took place on 22 July annually; St John's Eve (*Bealtaine*) was marked with hilltop bonfires; and the Feast of the Assumption was celebrated locally with what one writer termed 'the most disgusting drunkenness and debauchery'.[37] In 1844 the *Parliamentary gazetteer* gave the following account of a 'holy well' at Malin Head, just twelve miles (20km) north of Culdaff:

> it is reputed to possess a miraculous power of curing diseases and is consequently a serious nuisance to the neighbourhood; for it invites strollers and mendicants of the worst description from the three adjoining counties, who infest the neighbourhood by their numbers, and corrupt it by their example. The chief orgies at this well, as at many others in Ireland, are drunkenness and debauchery; and they assort so well with the corruption and ignorance of the mob, who see them sanctioned by superstition, that they have resisted the united efforts of Protestant and Roman Catholic for their suppression.[38]

This was a world into which the forces and structures of the centralized Victorian state obtruded, jostling alongside embedded traditions and beliefs, extended familial and neighbourhood relationships, and ad-hoc community-based means of dealing with disruption. With its imperial infrastructure – coastguard stations, Revenue Police barracks and the British military presence at Fort Dunree – and proximity to the city of Derry, Inishowen had been open to the influence of the English language from the early seventeenth-century Plantation of Ulster. In 1814 Chichester reported that in Culdaff the language spoken by the peasantry was English but the majority also spoke 'a patois, which is more nearly allied to Erse than to Irish'.[39] Despite his remarks, it is likely that prior to the Famine many of the ordinary people of Culdaff conducted their daily business through Irish. The number of Irish speakers declined nationally between 1830 and 1851 – likely in Inishowen, too – but the language remained ubiquitous in the western half of Ulster.[40] It has been estimated that of people born in the barony of east Inishowen in 1771–81, at least 50–9 per cent spoke Irish; of those born in 1861–71, the figure was less than 2 per cent.[41] That said, a cluster of Irish speakers endured in north Inishowen into the mid-nineteenth century.[42] In Clonmany in the 1860s and 1870s, people were entertained at the fireside by Irish-language song.[43] Revd Francis Lucas Molloy stated of that parish in *c.*1814:

> The vernacular language is what is used by the people in common, although they are acquiring a tolerable knowledge of English now, since their ideas were whetted by a commercial intercourse in the neighbouring fairs and markets. [...] some of the old men in this parish have a genius for reading the Irish language, in Irish characters [...] There are some old poems on Fion Mc Cuil, and many fragments of what they call Ossian's poems.[44]

Similarly, in adjacent Clonca, it was noted that

> Some older people [...] in the most remote parts [...] occasionally repeat poetical fragments like those translated by Mr McPherson and ascribed to him by Ossian. The Irish harp is unknown here; but some of the ancient national airs are occasionally sung. The mountain herds often sing a very wild kind of air.[45]

In his important memoir of growing up in Clonmany, McGlinchey related how in his early years Irish was widely spoken across the parish and would be heard at all gatherings and on fair days, but throughout the course of his life English came to the fore.[46] Families all over Ireland became aware of the advantages offered by a facility in English, and so generally did not discourage their children from speaking it. In the early 1960s Emrys Evans gathered testimonies from the few remaining native speakers in north-west Inishowen which he interpreted as indicating that the generation born in the 1880s and 1890s were raised in households in which Irish was the preserve of the parents and grandparents, a 'secret language' from which children were shielded.[47] In the census of 1881, just twenty-two people in the whole of Inishowen of Mary's generation (i.e., those aged 50–9, born around 1830) self-declared as monolingual Irish speakers, while 643 self-declared as bilingual. In the census of 1891, just sixteen people of the same generation (then aged 60–9) in east Inishowen self-declared as monolingual Irish speakers; in the same age cohort, 562 claimed to be bilingual in Irish and English. The census of 1901 records that the entire Inishowen peninsula contained just twenty-two monoglot Irish speakers over the age of 60 (i.e., those who were alive at the time of Mary's murder), while 1,150 of the same age group claimed to be bilingual. It is not known whether the individuals studied in this book spoke Irish or English or both, but the lack of comment to the contrary in the press indicates that Daniel McKeeny's trial was conducted in English; those who conducted legal business through Irish were frequently the subject of negative public commentary and indeed could be subjected to harsher cross-examination within the courtroom.[48]

National primary education was instituted in Ireland in 1831, guaranteeing free education for every child and an alternative to the fee-paying hedge schools like the one in Clonmany parish run by a man in his seventies who gave instruction in English, Irish, French, Latin and Greek.[49] One historian has referred to the 'general diffusion of reading, writing and arithmetic' in the course of the nineteenth century 'as the major, and perhaps the only, significant achievement of the system'.[50] Mary Doherty was part of the first generation of Irish Catholics to be born with access to education; Catholic schools were illegal in Ireland until 1782 and their financing remained restricted until 1829. Tremendous inequalities remained, however. For every one adult who could read and write in Culdaff parish in 1841, more than three could not.[51] Nationally, among men born in the 1820s, the literacy rate was around 45 per cent; for women born in the same decade, it was about 25 per cent.[52] Most children, and the vast majority of girls, did not remain in education beyond the age of 10 or 12, and Culdaff parish school was attended only by male pupils in 1837.[53] While this reflects the national trend until the 1840s, whereby the number of female pupils was half that of males, the county average for Donegal was better, with at least eight girls in school for every ten boys.[54] (Daniel McKeeny could read 'a little'.)[55] A third school was located in Carthage townland, across the road from Carthage House and a short walk from the farm where Mary Doherty worked as a servant. She may have watched other children going to and from the elongated roadside school building with envy. Or, perhaps, she may have been glad to be freed of the obligation to shiver daily in a cold schoolhouse threatened with corporal punishment, where intellectual development came in a far second behind the state goal of forging meek and hardworking citizens. An 1852 parliamentary report on Catholic education stated

> that the children of the poor should possess more or less knowledge of grammar or geography is really, in itself, a matter of very small concern either to themselves or to the state; but that they should be so trained as to become hereafter lovers of justice, purity, patience, and industry, to be, in a word, good men and good citizens – this is worthy of any expenditure, however costly, of any toil, however laborious.[56]

The west Inishowen Church of Ireland minister Francis Molloy noted that even when children learned 'little or nothing' at school, it kept them

> from bad practices and the contagion of bad examples [...] for if they were not at school, they would probably be in the streets, or in the church-yard, gaming for halfpence, quarrelling, robbing bird's-nests, and practising every vice of which their age is capable.[57]

Despite his negative remarks Molloy, a native of Co. Monaghan, knew the people of his parish well and was highly regarded for helping them find work and even offering shelter at the Rectory in times of dire need.[58]

The celebrated poet Frances Browne (1816–79) was a contemporary of Daniel McKeeny. While she grew up in Stranorlar, 48 miles (77km) south of Culdaff and in an economically and socially distinct region of Co. Donegal, her memories of local literacy are illuminating. She recalled, 'Books have always been scarce in our remote neighbourhood – and were much more so in my childhood'. She described the reading

6. Interior of an Inishowen farm kitchen. © National Museums Northern Ireland / Mary Evans.

material 'most common' in Stranorlar: *The history of Susan Gray* (1802) by popular children's writer Mary Martha Sherwood; *The gentle shepherd* (1725) by Scottish playwright Allan Ramsay; the travels of Scottish explorer Mungo Park; and Daniel Defoe's *Robinson Crusoe* (1719).[59] The preference for Scottish writers may reflect the strength of the Presbyterian faith and Ulster-Scots cultural identity in the Finn valley, as well as her own family's religious background, but her memories are nevertheless a useful barometer of the broader reading trends in rural Donegal in the decades preceding the Famine.

Alongside the difficulties and challenges of daily life, paying the rent and feeding large families, the people of Culdaff and the surrounding area enjoyed a range of entertainments. People, of course, found occasion for merriment and fun. The hearth was the functional and social centre of the home, where families gathered for meals, welcomed visitors, sang and played music (fig. 6).[60] This musical tradition was collected and published by Honoria Tomkins

Galwey (1830–1925), daughter of the rector of Moville.[61] Communal events included spring ploughing matches and celebrations at harvest time. Young recorded harvest merrymaking in Culdaff in October 1841:

> About 50 of the Glengad tenants came a 2nd day to the 'shearing' and cut down all the late oats. They had some whiskey, and a piper in the barn, and danced and sung to a late hour in great delight. We all went to see them, and were surprised by their good dancing, which they seemed to enjoy very much.[62]

In their three-volume work on Ireland, the oft-quoted travelling couple Samuel Carter and Anna Maria Hall described Inishowen as 'more primitive than any other portion of Ireland [...] of late [...] the coast from Moville round to Killybegs was famous for all that was rude, uncultivated and lawless'.[63] Inishowen economy and society were markedly different to those of neighbouring east-central Donegal to the south. Breandán Mac Suibhne and David Dickson have pointed out that the Fanad peninsula was subject to similarly negative characterizations because its 'proximity to an advantaged, heavily Protestant district [...] cast cultural difference in sharp relief'.[64] Inishowen did have its problems, however. The region suffered from limited economic opportunities and endemic poverty, contributing to rising emigration and the criminalization of the population in the late eighteenth and early nineteenth centuries. The peninsula was renowned for its illegal distilleries from the 1780s to the 1820s. The scale of the industry meant that Inishowen set the market price for barley in north Ulster, with large tracts of land forced into unnatural productivity by the lucrative grain trade. This trade – carried on between Culdaff Bay and the island of Islay in exchange for Scottish barley, herring and horses – invited a severe government response, resulting in violent clashes between the Revenue Police and locals. Fines levied were out of all proportion to the inhabitants' means; in the spring and summer assizes of 1814 and 1815, 153 fines were issued, totalling £3,825. The burden on the population was such that the minister at Clonca abandoned his intention of building a new church and glebe house.[65] In the event of the non-payment of fines, funding for the repair of roads and bridges was withheld, causing in the 1810s 'great injury' to the three main roads in Culdaff parish.[66] In 1824 a government report described the people of Inishowen as 'smugglers and distillers from their cradles'.[67] Revd Richard Hamilton testified that 'illicit distillation does prevail in all Ennishowen', adding that 'the produce of the land has fallen very much' and that conditions in the parish have 'been lately disturbed'.[68] In the context of the tithe wars, Revd John Canning reported a rapid increase in the agrarian agitation known as Whiteboyism; in 1835–6 the Poor Inquiry Survey noted that north Inishowen was one of the most disturbed districts in Ulster.[69] An anti-tithe meeting held in Carndonagh in 1837 attracted 16,000 people, demonstrating the extent to which people were becoming politicized by deprivation.[70] In April 1841 Young received a circular from the Yeomanry requesting that he send any ammunition to the nearest ordinance store for safe keeping.[71] Inishowen came to be well defended by civil and military forces. By 1840 the coast was ringed with military defences, from Neds Point battery and ordnance ground on the edge of Buncrana, and Fort Dunree just north of there – both defending the Swilly – to Greencastle Fort on the Foyle. Inland, there was a barracks at Carndonagh and an infantry barracks at Clonmany. Police stations at Moville and Clonmany, and Revenue Police barracks in Clonmany, Culdaff and Greencastle completed the web.[72] While there would be no railway connection to bring the forces of law and order into the peninsula at short notice until the late nineteenth century, cavalry reinforcements could ride from the barracks at Derry, as described by an eyewitness in 1827.[73]

Despite this backdrop of unrest and entrenched low-level criminality, Donegal as a whole had the lowest homicide rate of any county in Ireland in the 1840s.[74] So, when 14-year-old servant Mary Doherty was brutally beaten to death in Bunagee on a spring Sunday morning in 1844, local, national and British newspapers emphasized the shocking and unusual nature of the crime. The outcry did not last, however, and within days the victim's name was forgotten.

2. A dreadful crime

> A feeling of the utmost consternation and disgust at the dreadful crime pervades all classes, it is of so novel a character in this part of the country, and one of so atrocious and cold-blooded a description.
>
> 'Appalling Murder', *The Era*, 24 March 1844.

Sunday, 10 March 1844. Mary Doherty's employers, the McKeeny family, had gone to mass, leaving the 14-year-old servant alone in the house.[1] They returned, possibly having been gone as long as two-and-a-half hours, to find her bloodied body on the kitchen floor. Her throat had been cut, her skull fractured, and an attempt had been made to burn her remains. A storage chest had been broken open, and over 50 shillings were missing from it.

As best I can ascertain from contemporary sources including George Young's diary and newspaper reports, the events of that morning were as follows: Daniel McKeeny waited until the time when most of his family and neighbours would have already set out for mass, at least a twenty-minute walk for most of them. He then set out for his uncle's house, a five-minute walk away. At least three witnesses claimed to have seen him on the road: John Kearney, Jane McLoughlan and the son of a man named Moran. McKeeny entered the house, broke into a chest and stole 50 shillings. Interrupted by Mary while exiting through the main kitchen and living space, he attacked her, striking her on the head with a blunt object and slitting her throat with a knife (neither weapon seems to have been recovered during the investigation). Standing over her lifeless body on the kitchen floor, he panicked. He attempted to burn her remains in the fireplace. Her woollen clothing would have been slow to catch fire and probably only smouldered. His panic mounting and knowing that he needed to be far from the scene when mass ended, he ran to the well, scrubbing the blood from his hands. Then he noticed the bloodstain on the sleeve of his dark, mixed grey frock-coat; seizing a knife, he attempted to cut this section from his coat sleeve. The shillings hung heavy in his pockets. He hid the money in and around his father's house, in the thatch and under stones, and made his way into Culdaff to attempt to build an alibi for himself. He was seen on the road by a child of Nancy McKeeny (whose relationship to the accused has not been established). Reaching a friend's house in the village, did he threaten, bully or cajole the promise of an alibi? Was his demeanour uncharacteristically dark or quiet, or did he over-compensate with a carefree air? When the constabulary and Revenue Police officers reached his friend's door, did he try to run, or loudly protest his innocence? Taken directly to Culdaff police barracks, and from there to Lifford gaol five days later, he would never see his home – or, possibly, his family – again.

When the alarm was raised by James McKeeny, the landlord, George Young, was brought to examine the body and the crime scene. John Harvey of Malin Hall and Dr Layard arrived shortly afterwards, and the men held an inquest. Young and Harvey were the first to be informed of Mary's death because they were Justices of the Peace, or JPs. Generally, when a body was found, four people would turn up: a coroner, a policeman, a stipendiary magistrate (or RM, resident magistrate) and an ordinary magistrate (usually a local landlord who likely owned the property where the murder took place); 'They did not have to turn up; their doing so was a sign that they took their [unpaid] duties seriously'.[2] The role of JP was considered an honour, but it was also a means of keeping abreast of events in the community and applying a level of control over the population. As a later local historian put it, Harvey and Young 'ruled the countryside in no weak fashion' and the latter was 'arrogant but kindly, all-powerful in his own demesne'.[3] JPs were often landlords who approached both of these roles with a paternalistic attitude, making it their business to know what was happening in the community, mediating in disagreements and disputes, and generally overseeing the lives of the humble people eking out a living on their estates. Like many other towns and villages across the country, Culdaff was essentially the estate town of the Young family, administered paternalistically and hierarchically.[4] Richard McMahon has interpreted the rate of out-of-court settlements in provincial petty sessions courts as indicative of a high degree of acceptance of local opinion and 'wider community relations' by legal practitioners and the justice system.[5] It is also important to note that historians have identified a prevailing mistrust among the Irish people more generally towards the state in matters of justice; Oliver McDonagh writes that 'the legal system of the state was distrusted and abhorred'.[6] That said, more recent work by McMahon has demonstrated a 'conditional acceptance' of the law, including when it was seen to achieve a compromise between 'popular ideas of justice and the official law'.[7]

Young and Harvey conducted the initial inspection of the crime scene, with the police only stepping in afterwards to perform the manhunt and the arrest. The JPs quickly deduced that 19-year-old Daniel McKeeny was the prime suspect; that Mary must have interrupted him in the course of a robbery; and that he killed her to avoid identification. He had been accused previously of sheep-stealing and was, in the words of a *Londonderry Sentinel* reporter, 'a noted bad character'.[8] He knew that his cousin, the son of Mary's employer, kept savings in the house, and that Mary's brother had recently sent her money from America.[9] Such intimate personal information was commonly shared in tight-knit communities, where the contents of an envelope from abroad was an object of speculation and letters were read aloud for the benefit of the illiterate.

Mary Doherty's date and place of birth are unknown, as are her parentage and family circumstances.[10] It is likely that she died close to where she was born and raised. Eight households in Carthage townland were headed by people named Doherty in 1855, but the predominance of this family name across Inishowen cautions against drawing any firm conclusions. A surname distribution search shows that in the late 1850s 1,721 households in Co. Donegal were headed by a person of that name – more than all other counties of Ireland combined.[11] While the facts of her life remain hidden, hers was not a life without meaning. She had at least one brother who cared enough to send her a remittance from America. Mary's brother's move to America took place in the context of rapidly rising emigration driven by rising food prices, falling farm earnings and evictions that displaced the poorest.[12] Around 1.5 million people left the island of Ireland in the years 1815–45, a million of whom went to the US.[13] In pre-Famine Ireland, however, emigration was rarely a viable option for the poorest in society, the landless or the jobless; prior to the establishment of assistance schemes, emigrants were more likely to be from farming or trading families.[14] Still, in the absence of other evidence, it cannot be assumed that Mary's brother was not one of the minority of desperately poor Irish who managed to find a means of crossing the Atlantic. Despite its relative geographical isolation, Culdaff was connected to the wider world by maritime trade and migration routes. Ships plying the route from Derry to North America passed within sight of the high ground surrounding Culdaff Bay. In spring 1841, for example, locals observed the ship *Erin* approaching the Foyle on its return journey from the US to Derry.[15] In February 1843, fragments of the *Salus* of Greenock, wrecked off Inishtrahull Island during severe weather en route to Honduras, washed ashore on Culdaff beach.[16] It is no stretch to suggest that Mary's brother left from Derry to make a new life in North America, as an important centre of transatlantic trade and a thriving hub of migrant traffic. By the 1830s, in the context of rising emigration rates, the port of Derry became one of the most important points of embarkation for Irish migrants to Canada; from there, many travelled onward to the US.[17] Mary's brother may have intended her to join him there; chain migration was common, whereby those who had already emigrated sent money home to fund family members' passages.

We can also piece together what Mary's daily life may have been like as a servant for a small farming family. Fourteen now seems a tender age to be employed in service, as Mary was when she died. The 1841 census recorded that 501 girls aged under 15 years, and 4,224 women aged 15 and over, were employed as domestic servants in Co. Donegal. Mary may have been forced into such work by the loss of one or both parents, or she may have simply come from a poor family with too many mouths to feed. She may also have been related to the McKeenys; 'servants' on small rural farms were frequently elderly or orphaned relatives of the householder (note that to be 'orphaned' in the nineteenth century could mean the death, or absence by emigration or other cause, of a child's parents or other relatives). One unverified source states that James McKeeny was Mary's uncle, but as this information was not noted in any other source, this was likely an error by the clerk who transcribed the original document.[18]

Servants and labourers employed on farms of all sizes were often treated quite badly. The fact that Mary did not attend mass with the McKeenys on the morning that she died is surprising, given the importance of Lenten devotion. It suggests that they may not have treated her kindly, despite the hugely valuable and physically demanding labour she would have performed in their household and on their farm. (Alternatively, was her presence in the house on Sunday 10 March an anomaly – did Daniel McKeeny choose mass time to commit the robbery because he expected the house to be empty?) Female servants worked solo in the household as 'maids-of-all-work', meaning they were expected to cover a wide range of duties and jobs. Typically, they would rise at dawn (or earlier on dark winter mornings) to light the fire – nothing could be done until then – and set a pot of porridge to cook for the family. Throughout the day, she would have helped with the care of any children or elderly or infirm members of the household, kept the fire, gathered eggs from the poultry, churned, fetched water from the well, washed and mended clothes, and prepared and cooked meals. Indeed, potatoes were such a labour-intensive crop to grow, harvest and prepare that a contemporary observer noted that women 'can never be clean or diligent in other matters until the nature of their food be changed'.[19] Mary's labour was vital to daily life in the McKeeny household, and it is likely that James McKeeny's wife – if she was still living; James McKeeny was a widower by 1866[20] – used the time saved on chores and cooking to augment the family income by spinning or through another 'home' industry. A contemporary source from Co. Down noted that 'a woman with four children "could not do more than keep the home and family clean; she could not make as much [by her own labour] as would buy soap to wash the children's clothes"'.[21] Then there were the annually ritualized, seasonal demands of the farm: sowing and harvesting grain and root crops, lambing, saving the turf, haymaking. Mary may have gathered wrack on the shore for use as fertilizer, or cleaned and prepared fish or seafowl for family meals. In the evenings, the family may have gathered together in the main room of the house, in the warmth of the turf fire, for storytelling or music; the women may have knitted or darned while being entertained. Chichester recorded in 1814 that 'a custom prevails for young women to assemble at spinning parties, to which each of them brings a wheel, for the purpose of enjoying society without impairing their industry'.[22] Overall, as demonstrated by Mary Cullen

– and as noted by Harriet Martineau visiting from England, 'it is the industry of women which is in great part sustaining the country'[23] – women's work and their contributions to household income were key to the survival of the labouring family, not only through the exhausting round of daily food preparation or contributing to the household income with earnings from 'cottage' or 'home' industries like spinning, but through the high-value work of rearing pigs and poultry. In Cullen's words, women's contributions to household income – which reached as much as 37 per cent – 'bridged the gap between comfort and distress, and [were] an important factor in the family's standard of living and in the difference between surviving and failing to survive by independent labour'.[24] Charles McGlinchey, born in 1861, recalled how his mother churned butter, carded wool and wove linen by the light of the fire.[25] Mary died in those early months of the year when supplies from the last harvest were dwindling, and in the third week of Lent; weddings and other celebrations would have been on hold for the period of observance, but she may have enjoyed a little additional food on Shrove Tuesday (20 February 1844) as part of the pre-Lenten tradition of feasting on dairy and eggs. In the days prior to her death, morning temperatures hovered around 0–3 degrees Celsius, with daytime highs of 7 degrees, as the sun only slowly edged towards earlier rising: hard times for the labouring poor and small family farmers.[26]

We know a lot more about Daniel McKeeny. Insights into his life and personality, as well as his physical appearance were recorded by the judicial and penal authorities. He was 5ft 6in (1.68m) tall with hazel eyes, brown hair and a 'fresh' complexion. He had an 'oval' face, no whiskers, a small forehead, large nose, freckles, a lancet mark on his right arm, and – indicating a life of hard work – he was missing the nail from his left thumb.[27] He could not write and could read 'a little'. His parents were named William ('Billy') and Kitty, and his siblings were Jacky (or John), William, Betty and Kitty.[28] Prior to Mary's murder, Daniel had gained a reputation in the locality; he had been accused of, but not brought before the courts for, sheep-stealing in July 1843. He appears to have been an opportunist – he stole his neighbour's ewe and lamb in time for the fair day in Carndonagh, where he probably hoped to dispose of the animals quickly. Similarly, he carried out the botched burglary on his uncle's house on a Sunday morning, probably expecting the house to be empty. His actions appear rash, however, given the eyewitnesses who reported seeing him bringing the ewe and lamb to market, and those who informed the police and the landlord that they saw him going towards his uncle's house at a time when others were making their way to mass.

The extended McKeeny family was well-established in Bunagee (or at least no less so than most of their neighbours). The Tithe Applotment Books, compiled for the civil (Church of Ireland) parish of Culdaff in 1827–8, name the occupiers of land in the townland of Carthage, which included Bunagee at the time (see table 3).[29] The accompanying maps do not survive and so it is unfortunately not possible to link those occupiers to later generations of the McKeeny family, or to know which branch of the family occupied which plot of land. It also emphasizes one of the great frustrations of Irish family history research: the re-use of first names within and across generations of the same family. It is not possible to say with certainty, for example, whether either of the two Daniels listed in the Tithe Applotment Books is a father, uncle or other relative of the Daniel McKeeny who would be accused of the murder of Mary Doherty sixteen years later.

Both the Tithe Applotment Books and *Griffith's valuation* of 1855 demonstrate that some of the extended McKeeny family lived in a clachan – a cluster of dwellings, farm buildings and land – in the heart of Bunagee (table 3). In 1855 three households (44a, 44b and 44c) shared one subdivided plot of land, characteristic of clachan living. Charles McGonigle (44a) married Bridget McKeeny in 1852; this branch of the family appears to have become extinct in 1934. Mary McKeeny headed the household at 44b in 1855, and Thomas McKeeny the plot at 44c; it is not possible to state with certainty which of these households Daniel McKeeny may have belonged to. A few hundred metres to the west, separate from the cluster and set apart from the rest of the extended family, was James McKeeny's (*c.*1776–1866), the house and farm where Mary Doherty worked and was killed (no. 42); and, a little to the north, the house and land of another Daniel McKeeny (no. 37); again, it is not possible to state with certainty whether this was the convict's homeplace. In between the McKeenys, at no. 43, lived Philip and Sarah Cornish and their small family of at least two daughters (Sarah, born *c.*1836, and Mary, born *c.*1839).[30] James McKeeny's plot sat at the westernmost part of Bunagee/Carthage, bordering the townland of Muff, on a slightly elevated site bounded by a large oval area of rough ground.

Table 3. McKeeny family occupiers of land in Carthage townland. Spellings and plot numbers are presented as given in the original sources. It is not possible to match the plot numbers of the different sources as the maps made in the 1827–8 survey have not survived

<table>
<tr><th>Plot no.</th><th>Occupier</th><th>Acres Roods Perches</th><th>Land Valuation</th><th>Buildings Valuation</th><th>Total Valuation</th><th>Tithe</th></tr>
<tr><td colspan="7">1827–8</td></tr>
<tr><td>510</td><td>James McKeeny</td><td rowspan="4">32.0.3</td><td>-</td><td>-</td><td rowspan="4">19.3.3</td><td rowspan="4">2.6.3</td></tr>
<tr><td>511</td><td>Patrick McKeeny</td><td>-</td><td>-</td></tr>
<tr><td>512</td><td>Thomas McKeeny</td><td>-</td><td>-</td></tr>
<tr><td>513</td><td>William McKeeny</td><td>-</td><td>-</td></tr>
<tr><td>514</td><td>John McKinny</td><td rowspan="3">38.2.31</td><td>-</td><td>-</td><td rowspan="3">12.10.5</td><td rowspan="3">1.10.3</td></tr>
<tr><td>515</td><td>William McKinny</td><td>-</td><td>-</td></tr>
<tr><td>516</td><td>Patrick McKinny</td><td>-</td><td>-</td></tr>
<tr><td>536</td><td>Daniel McKeeney</td><td>28.0.14</td><td>-</td><td>-</td><td>1.8.8</td><td>0.3.5</td></tr>
<tr><td>547</td><td>Daniel McKeeney</td><td>22.2.9</td><td>-</td><td>-</td><td>15.9.1</td><td>1.17.5</td></tr>
<tr><td colspan="7">1855</td></tr>
<tr><td>37</td><td>Daniel McKeeny</td><td>18.1.35</td><td>5.5.0</td><td>0.15.0</td><td>6.0.0</td><td>-</td></tr>
<tr><td>42</td><td>James McKeeny</td><td>10.0.10</td><td>0.15.0</td><td>1.0.0</td><td>7.15.0</td><td>-</td></tr>
<tr><td>44a</td><td>Charles McGonigle*</td><td rowspan="3">43.0.5</td><td>4.5.0</td><td>0.10.0</td><td>4.15.0</td><td>-</td></tr>
<tr><td>44b</td><td>Mary McKeeny</td><td>4.5.0</td><td>0.10.0</td><td>4.15.0</td><td>-</td></tr>
<tr><td>44c</td><td>Thomas McKeeny</td><td>8.10.0</td><td>1.0.0</td><td>9.10.0</td><td>-</td></tr>
</table>

Sources: Tithe Applotment Books (1827–8), NLI; *Griffith's valuation*, 1855.
*Married to Bridget McKeeny. Valuations in £ *s. d.*

Daniel's uncle, James – Mary's employer – appears to have been slightly better-off than most of his neighbours. A national survey of rateable property carried out in 1847–64 shows that only six plots in the townland were valued higher than James McKeeny's.[31] The land was not of very good quality, however – mostly what the Ordnance Survey categorized as 'rough pasture'.[32] The valuation of the family home suggests its similarity to the vast majority of dwellings in Carthage: a one- or two-roomed cabin with thatched roof. The first-edition Ordnance Survey map (1834) depicts a typical long, narrow dwelling on a rectangular plan with two outbuildings nearby, and a lime kiln. Typically, the interior of the single-storey house would have been 'divided into apartments each of which occupies the full width of the house and each opens into the next and not into a central hallway or passage', with the kitchen area in the middle.[33] In terms of their separate holdings of 10–18 acres, the extended branches of the McKeeny family fell just within the lower limit of being able to plan for the future.[34] The fact that Daniel McKeeny robbed his own cousin hints at some possible resentment, jealousy or ill feeling. It is easy to imagine how such feelings could emerge between members of an extended family living in close quarters, but in quite different material circumstances, as indicated by James McKeeny's son's reserve of 50 shillings.[35]

Given his resources, did James McKeeny give Mary a wake, a funeral, a headstone? Perhaps there was a wake, with keening and the 'unbounded mirth and festivity' of the traditional games played on such occasions in pre-Famine rural Ireland, but George Young's otherwise detailed diary makes no mention of a funeral for the girl.[36] Perhaps she was interred in the cemetery attached to the relatively new parish church at Bocan, perched on high ground overlooking flatlands to Trawbreaga Bay, or in the shadow of Aughaclay's older parish church; parish burial records from the time of her death have not survived, and no memorial remains bearing her name.

3. Bringing home the guilt

> It is hoped that evidence may transpire to bring home the guilt to the perpetrator of the brutal act.
>
> 'Horrible murder in Ennishowen',
> *Londonderry Journal*, 19 March 1844.

Daniel McKeeny was arrested in an unspecified house in Culdaff on the day of the murder by Revenue Police sub-officer William McNutt and Constable Henderson of the Irish Constabulary.[1] The Revenue Police was established to combat illicit distillation, a task they executed so successfully that the organization was disbanded in 1857.[2] Of the eleven counties first allocated Revenue Police stations in 1833, Donegal had by far the most at seventeen.[3] Col. William Brereton, commander of the force, later recalled:

> I went over the whole of Ireland, and over every square mile almost of it before making my proposal to the Treasury, and thus became acquainted with those parts of Ireland that actually required parties […] I placed nearly one-third of the whole force in the county of Donegal, and that part of the county of Derry that is nearest to it.[4]

McNutt was among the first group of trained privates to emerge from the Irish Revenue Police training depot in Clonliffe, Dublin, in late 1836, and was initially assigned to Stranorlar station; it is not known when he moved to Malin (the station that served Culdaff).[5] Recruits had to meet strict educational and family conditions depending on the rank at which they sought to join the force; all recruits had to be able to read and write and be numerically literate.[6] As a sub-officer, McNutt was at the highest non-commissioned rank in the Irish Revenue Police. The role included a wide range of responsibilities in addition to having charge of the station party:

> [the sub-officer] had to observe all the regulations prescribed for lieutenants [...] where there was no sergeant attached to his party, the sub-officer was also to be guided by the orders that were laid down for the observance of sergeants as to the care of barracks, furniture, clothing, arms etc.; informing privates of their duties; keeping a correct roster; parading and inspecting the party before proceeding on duty; calling the roll at night; keeping the mess accounts; and properly managing the mess (but he was not to mess with the party). [...] The sub-officer was not authorized to arrest persons, except those detected in offences declared as such by the 19th, 25th and 30th sections of 1 & 2, Will. IV, c. 44, with which act the sub-officer was to make himself thoroughly acquainted.[7]

McNutt would have had a fair standard of living, particularly in comparison to most of the family farmers and labourers in Culdaff parish. In 1853 sub-officers earned between 2*s*. 6*d*. and 3*s*. 6*d*. per day; all ranks slept in the barracks and were fed there; every officer was given a suit of clothes each year; and station parties were rewarded with a prize of £2 2*s*. per prisoner arrested and convicted, to be divided between the men. In 1857 the supplies given to each officer comprised a blue cloth 'frock' (uniform); a pair of Oxford grey cloth trousers; a sword, sword knot and belt; a shako (a tall military cap); a forage cap; a portable iron bedstead; a hair mattress; three blankets, one quilt and two pairs of sheets; two pillows; and a printed cloth valise to contain their bedding.[8]

The Irish Constabulary (later Royal Irish Constabulary), like the Revenue Police, laid down strict entry requirements for recruits. In the 1840s, these included the possession of 30*s*. in savings, two pairs of strong boots, three good shirts and four pairs of stockings[9] – requirements that put a career in policing out of reach of the majority of Irish men. Furthermore, they had to be aged between 19 and 27 and be unmarried or a widower without children; they could seek permission to marry after seven years' service.[10] Women of all classes were excluded. Policing offered steady work at a competitive rate of pay, especially in comparison to labourers' wages – a sub-constable's starting salary was £24 per annum in 1836 – but everyday duties were unenviable (ranging from prosecuting the owners of straying

7. Main Street, Culdaff, with site of police barracks to right (courtesy of National Museums Northern Ireland/Mary Evans).

livestock to enforcing liquor sales laws) and could contribute to an individual officer's unpopularity in his locality.[11]

McKeeny was held in Culdaff police barracks. The two-storey terraced building on the south side of the main street (fig. 7) was home to the constabulary force from its establishment in 1827 until 1869, when they moved directly across the street. Sited on the slightly rising ground of Culdaff village, the officers would have had a good view from the rear of the building of the surrounding boggy countryside to the south and south-west.

The investigation that took place into Mary Doherty's murder is unrecognizable in comparison to the process of building a case even by the end of the nineteenth century. Without fingerprinting, photography, telegram or other means of gathering and communicating information quickly, the investigation and the case depended on reputable, reliable eyewitnesses who were willing to testify. George Young appears to have been heavily involved in the investigation, such as it was, and the building of the case against McKeeny. He recorded in his diary that on 11 March he was 'busy taking additional evidence about the murder which make [*sic*] the case against D. McKeeny still more suspicious'.[12] (Regrettably, he does not indicate what that evidence may have been.) He attempted to recreate McKeeny's steps on the day of the murder, having a child of Nancy McKeeny show him where he passed the accused on the road that day, and received hearsay information from Philip Cornish to the effect that two other men – James Kearney and the son of a man named Moran – had seen McKeeny 'going to' his uncle's house 'shortly before the murder'.[13] On 25 March Young engaged a Mr Craig to make a 'sketch' of Bunagee and the neighbouring townland of Muff 'to explain the scene of the late murder', and on 28 March he gathered together 'all the inhabitants […] for half a mile round' in the village Loan Fund office and 'gained some strong additional evidence against Donl. McKeeney [*sic*]'.[14] On the morning of Sunday 31 March, before church, he walked to the new Bunagee Road 'to examine more particularly into some points concerning Donl. McKeeny's movements on the day of the murder'.[15] The case then fades from view in his diary until 3 May, when he had 'another investigation […] in consequence of 5/– [shillings] having been found in Billy McKeeny's turf stack'.[16] The following day, John Harvey sent Young a copy of a letter McKeeny had written to his father, with instructions to search for a sovereign (equal to 20 shillings) he had hidden in the roof of their house; Young directed the police to search for it, but the money was not recovered.[17] On 12 June, a map was made of Bunagee, 'showing the various tracks taken by Donl. McKeeny on the day of the murder, as proved in the several informations'.[18]

Despite these efforts, in the absence of eyewitnesses to the killing or, it seems, a murder weapon, the entire case against McKeeny appears to have hinged on one question. It was reported that during interview with his arresting officers McKeeny said that he had been at mass at the time of the murder, but his named alibis denied having been in his company.[19] Similarly, Young noted that prior to his arrest, McKeeny gave him 'a different account from the true one, of his having gone to chapel'.[20] At a time when 700–1400 people were estimated to have attended weekly services in Bocan parish chapel, a face could easily have been missed in the crowd; that said, it could be assumed that regular mass-goers would have established spots within the church where they habitually sat or stood, meaning a presence or absence could easily be noted.[21] McKeeny's untruthfulness and his shaken alibi were taken as confirmation of his guilt and on Friday 15 March he was conveyed to Lifford gaol to await trial on charges of murder and sheep-stealing.[22]

Almost 40 miles (64km) south of Culdaff, in the rich, fertile farmland lying between the Rivers Finn and Foyle, sits Lifford: the county town, the centre of administration in Donegal. The grim, imposing façades of the gaol and courthouse loomed over the small market town, which consisted of just three streets.[23] The gaol sat at the heart of a cluster of administrative buildings located prominently, surrounding the main square on three sides: the gaol to the north, the asylum and courthouse to the east, and the County House to the west. Far from the moral and physiological contagion of those institutions, at the opposite end of the town, lay the infirmary.

Built beside the courthouse in 1793 to accommodate up to 124 prisoners and replace the damp, dark, vaulted jail in the basement of the mid-eighteenth-century courthouse – described in 1843 as 'very ill-calculated indeed for the Reception of any Persons'[24] – Lifford gaol's squat but forbidding castellated exterior was the backdrop to public executions until 1847.[25] It was built to the standard plan employed across Britain and Ireland, the U-shaped prisoners' quarters facing into a T-shaped administrative building to maximize surveillance and control. From inside the three-storey gaol, prisoners may have observed people going about their lives on the outside: people fishing on the River Finn flowing by just metres away, perhaps, or squealing children playing and running on the street.

Strict rules were enforced within the prison walls. Common minor infractions such as 'speaking in Irish contrary to the regulations', failure to keep their own clothing or beds clean and tidy, swearing, 'idling' or being found in possession of tobacco, were all punishable by withholding of milk rations for periods of one to three days.[26] There were repeated examples of prisoners being punished for sharing their own rations with a fellow inmate who had been placed on reduced rations.[27] Prisoners were placed in solitary confinement for 'irreverent conduct in chapel', refusing to break stones, and for fighting.[28] On the day of McKeeny's first appearance in Lifford courthouse in July

1844, Judge Robert Torrens (1775–1856) stated in open court that Judge Louis Perrin (1782–1864) reported to him that within Lifford gaol was 'a dungeon without any light, in which prisoners sentenced to solitary confinement were put, and that he considered such a place of confinement highly objectionable'. The foreman responded that the matter had been reported to the committee of the gaol and that they had 'in the most prompt manner given orders to have the grievance remedied, and that in future the building which was used as the chapel, and which was well lighted, should be converted into three solitary cells'.[29] (It was not suggested what part of the gaol might thereafter serve as a place of worship.) The roughness of life in the gaol is indicated by the constant stream of minor infractions and inter-prisoner conflict noted in the turnkeys' reports; governors' rules about order and deportment appear to have been the expression of an unattainable ideal, rather than reflective of any reality on the ground. Fights, rows and disagreements between prisoners were a regular occurrence. On several separate occasions, prisoners had their milk rations withheld for a day for 'exposing [themselves] in the privy'.[30] And while the strict rules about personal cleanliness appear to have been rigorously enforced, it is hard to imagine that men and women engaged in hard labour while subsisting on minimal rations had the energy to do much beyond emptying their own slop-bucket. Lewis's *Topographical dictionary* recorded in 1837 that the male prisoners were employed in breaking stones and 'pounding bones for manure' while the women were made to spin, sew and launder.[31] It was here and in these circumstances that Daniel McKeeny awaited trial for murder for four months, from 15 March until the next assizes on 19 July.

The twice-yearly Lifford assizes – where cases of murder and other serious crimes were heard – brought crowds to the small riverside town, and much-needed business to local boarding houses and taverns.[32] Young travelled to Lifford two days in advance, on 17 July, and dined with the other members of the Grand Jury, which included prominent Donegal landholders such as Lord George Hill of Gweedore (23,000 acres).[33] People travelled long distances to attend assizes, markets and fairs, which were great occasions for socializing and exchanging news. Assizes were big occasions; a contemporary eyewitness described judges walking in procession to the courthouse of a country town: 'First came a trumpeter and a mounted policeman riding abreast, then two policemen, then two troopers; then came the judges' carriage [...] then two more troopers, followed by two more mounted police'.[34] It is not difficult to imagine, against this exciting backdrop, folk theorizing about Mary's murder, fuelled by speculation about details such as McKeeny's bloodstained coat sleeve. These topics would have provided great fodder for an animated evening's discussion in Lifford's inns and public houses. Indeed, Margaret Kelleher recounts how locals in Maamtrasna, Co. Galway, 'relayed key pieces of information to each another' in the immediate aftermath of the murder of a family of five there in 1882, with rumours spreading while people went about their work at the turf.[35]

On the afternoon of Friday 19 July Judge Torrens took his seat in the Crown Court. The Grand Jury – twenty-three of the county's wealthiest and most prominent residents – had completed their meeting, approving spending on improvements to roads, bridges and public buildings across the county and, having been sworn in, were ready to consider the criminal cases. As summer light flooded through the high-ceilinged courtroom's large, south-facing windows, did the reporters and interested public gathered in the balcony squint to make out the figures in the dock? Public interest in court proceedings more generally is indicated by an incident that took place in Lifford Record Court on the same day. While one of the cases was being heard, a police officer roughly handled two men who separately attempted to enter the courtroom, employing his baton on the second, 'a plain-looking countryman'. Judge Perrin noticed the disturbance and directed the sheriff to place the officer in custody. Coming before the bench, the officer apologized and stated that he was following the sheriff's orders 'to prevent persons from crowding the seats'. The judge stated that 'he could not believe the sheriff had given such orders, and, if it was the case, he was acting beyond his authority. That it was a public court, and he would allow no man to use such violence to an unoffending person'. He ordered that the constable be removed from duty.[36] The incident demonstrates that the public were interested in attending legal proceedings, and that overcrowding could be an issue in courtrooms.

On Judge Torrens's docket that day were cases of 'riot and affray', an assault by riding on horseback over a person causing their death, obstruction of excise officers, a range of thefts (of livestock, money and property), and conspiracy to murder. Torrens opened proceedings by addressing the courtroom, attributing the (on the whole) 'happy and tranquil' state of Co. Donegal to the presence of the members of the Grand Jury, whose landed interests rendered them vigilant in the preservation of the peace. He stated that the cases before them that day were 'extremely light',[37] but drew their attention to one exception – the charge of homicide against McKeeny, explaining that 'in this case, the crown, finding the evidence not sufficiently clear to bring the guilt home to the accused person, thought it preferable not to bring it now before you, but suspend it for further investigation'.[38] (The *Ballyshannon Herald* noted that McKeeny was separately charged with the theft of two sheep.)[39] McKeeny's trial was postponed by eight months, until the next assizes on 18 March 1845. That morning, before proceedings opened, Young met with Judge Torrens and consulted with the crown lawyers, noting in his diary that they decided to put off McKeeny's trial until the next assizes, in the hope of getting further evidence.[40] The accused himself would not testify, address the court or be questioned or cross-examined on either occasion; until 1898, those answering to criminal charges were deemed 'incompetent' and therefore were not permitted to testify in court.[41]

Also in the dock at the Lifford assizes of 19 July was 27-year-old farm labourer Michael Gallagher. He was found guilty of 'having in his possession two heifers [...] which had been stolen from Francis Flood' in December 1843, for which Judge Torrens sentenced him to ten years' transportation.[42] Flood (1775–1859) was occupier of 123 acres at Heneys, two miles (3.2km) north of Donegal town, leased from John Hamilton of St Ernan's (1800–84); the land and buildings were given an annual valuation of £33 and £3 10*s*. respectively, and he was the thirty-fourth most propertied person in his parish of Killymard in terms of acreage.[43] Others sentenced to transportation that day were James Clark (seven years) for the theft of clothing and a watch; Peter Coyle (fifteen years) for robbery; and Henry Scott (seven years) for stealing two shirts.[44]

Three weeks after the trial, on 5 August, Michael Gallagher made a statement to the board of Lifford gaol. He claimed that while rooming together in the gaol, Daniel McKeeny had confided in him the following information: that Daniel had waited for James McKeeny to leave the house, then raped Mary and murdered her for fear of her complaint; that he struck her with a hammer and cut her throat; that he washed the blood from his hands so 'severely' with sand and water that his hand became swollen; that he cut a bloodstain from his coat sleeve and burnt it, and then burnt the rest of the coat; that he took 50 shillings from a chest in his uncle's house, hiding some in his father's turf stack and some 'under a stone on the sea side' (which McKeeny later allegedly wrote from gaol to ask his brother to retrieve); and that he was guilty of stealing sheep from Philip Cornish.[45]

On that same day, 5 August, Gallagher petitioned the lord lieutenant, calling into question the veracity of the prosecution witness in his own case. This man, James Travers, he claimed, was a man 'of infamous and proverbially bad character'. He also stated that he had been advised in bad faith by the brother-in-law of the complainant not to go to the expense of calling witnesses on his own behalf, to support his claim that he had actually purchased the two cows he was accused of stealing. He also appealed for the viceroy's mercy as the sole breadwinner for a young family and an aged dependant (his mother) who were doomed to 'utter ruin, poverty and distress'. His petition was supported by a testimonial from his parish priest in Templecarn; priests and MPs often lent their voices to such appeals.[46]

On 15 August Revd Edward Marmaduke Clarke (1794–1863) provided a gaol chaplain's perspective on the matter.[47] He stated that Gallagher had every opportunity of communicating with McKeeny when the pair shared a cell. There was also a high probability that Gallagher had heard the particulars of McKeeny's case from another prisoner or during one of his wife's visits. Clarke confirmed that Mary Doherty's murder had been 'the subject of public rumour', including specifics such as the question of whether McKeeny had burned his coat, where he had hidden the money and whether it had been found. Clarke also discovered that Gallagher's wife, Mary, knew the owner of the lodgings where witnesses stayed during the trial, and that she had visited and conversed with them. He stated that Mary visited Michael after the assizes and that the couple had a 'long and earnest conversation' that Michael interrupted to deliver his statement to the authorities. Clarke questioned why Gallagher waited until Tuesday to communicate a confession that he had allegedly heard on Sunday, and why, having delayed, did he interrupt a visit to do so? He concluded, 'Is it in the least probable that McKeeny with such a charge impending would make such a confession, as few men, even if fully acquitted of the charge, would dare to make to a fellow man?'[48] Clarke was referring to the death sentence McKeeny faced in the event of a guilty verdict.

The local landowners and JPs, George Young and John Harvey, were also involved in investigating Gallagher's claim. On 16 August Young received a letter from Edward Tierney (1780–1856), crown solicitor for the North West (Donegal) Circuit, enclosing a copy of Gallagher's information against McKeeny.[49] Young wrote from Culdaff House on 17 August to confirm that Harvey had interviewed McKeeny's brother John (or Jacky), who denied having found the allegedly hidden money. John McKeeny had heard about Michael Gallagher's claims and stated that when he visited Daniel in prison, Gallagher had questioned him about the murder. But, as Young pointed out, 'every particular concerning the murder was so well known all over the country that I have no doubt Gallagher could very easily have become acquainted with them without having heard anything of the matter from the prisoner himself'. Young planned to interview John but felt that nothing would come of Gallagher's information because it was at variance with the post-mortem results and contradicted the evidence of all sworn witnesses as to McKeeny's clothing on the day of the murder.[50] Gallagher stated that McKeeny told him 'that he cut the bloody sleeve off the coat and burned it, and least it might lead to his [*ink blot*] he burned the coat', but witnesses stated and reconfirmed to Young in August 1844 that McKeeny was wearing the same dark frock coat of mixed grey both before and after the time of the murder.[51] What shape Young's interview with John McKeeny took, where it took place, what questions were asked and how they were answered, all remain a mystery. The only record is Young's report which filters the event, silences the second party to the conversation and presents the information at a remove, not even paraphrazing but summarizing in the briefest manner what John related. The following is Young's entire account of the interview:

> [I] sent for John McKeeny the prisoner's brother who denied having found the two pounds in question – He had previously

> heard the report of Gallagher's having sworn informations and told me that when he had first gone to Lifford to see his brother a short time after his committal he had some conversation with Gallagher who asked him several questions relative to the murder – and in fact every particular concerning the murder was so well known all over the country that I have no doubt Gallagher could very easily have become acquainted with them without having heard anything of the matter from the prisoner himself. I shall however again examine the prisoner's brother more particularly and let you know the result.[52]

It has not been possible to ascertain whether the follow-up interview took place, or what additional information it furnished, if any.

Young enclosed with this letter a concise report in response to specific queries posed by Tierney. The document details the landowner and JP's knowledge of the case. It tells us that Dr Layard performed Mary's post-mortem and found no evidence of rape, but did find a 'deep wound about 5 or 6 inches in length on the right side of the throat [...] also a severe wound or bruise on her forehead'. It describes a swelling observed on the back of McKeeny's hand at the time of his arrest that 'had not the appearance of having been rubbed with sand' (as per Gallagher's claim) and the dark frock coat of mixed grey worn by McKeeny when seen in the morning by John Kearney and Jane McLoughlan, and which witnesses said he was still wearing after the murder. Finally, Young stated that he had made a 'strict' but unsuccessful search for the original of a letter McKeeny sent to his brother referring to the hidden money (and of which Young had a copy, no longer extant).[53]

Crown solicitor Tierney reviewed Gallagher's appeal on 2 September, following consultations with Clarke and Young. Tierney referred to the latter as having 'taken a great deal of pains to ascertain the facts connected with this case, the crime having been committed on his property'. The crown solicitor's assessment of Gallagher's claim focused on the alleged confession of rape. Reviewing the case, Tierney reiterated that the post-mortem examination found no sign of sexual assault. He concluded that Gallagher fabricated the confession in an attempt to secure his own liberty.[54]

On 10 August Judge Torrens responded to Michael Gallagher's petition from the comfort of his grand residence, Derrynoid Lodge at Tobermore near Derry. Antipathy dripped from his pen:

> I do not consider the prisoner a proper object for a mitigation of punishment – the allegations in his memorial are altogether groundless. He was convicted as well on his own confession, as by the testimony of two unimpeachable witnesses. [...] There could not be a clearer case for conviction and punishment.[55]

Torrens was a native of Derry, the son and grandson of churchmen. He was a stern character motivated by fundamentalist Christian ideals; at the Tyrone assizes in 1853, he delayed an execution to allow convicted murderer Alexander Mullan one month to 'profit by clerical instruction in the interval'.[56] An obituary stated that 'in the administration of criminal justice he was somewhat severe, particularly during his first years on the bench, when the disturbed state of the country, with overflowing assizes and constant commissions, afforded scope for a vigour not always within the law'.[57] In line with his initial judgment and his review of the case, Gallagher was transported to Van Diemen's Land on 15 February 1845.

Fifty-three weeks after the murder of Mary Doherty, on 14 March 1845, Daniel McKeeny stood in the dock in Lifford courthouse once more, this time before Chief Justice John Doherty (1783–1850). Dublin-born Doherty was called to the Bar in 1808, was a Member of Parliament in 1824–30, and was appointed solicitor-general in 1827. In both of these roles, he and Daniel O'Connell clashed swords, with the latter believing that Doherty was unfit for the bench. Doherty resigned his seat in parliament when he was appointed lord chief justice of the common pleas for Ireland in 1830.[58]

In the eight months that had passed since the summer assizes of 1844 the crown prosecution, seemingly reliant on circumstantial evidence – indeed, a report published just five days after the murder stated that there was 'a chain of circumstantial evidence' against 'a young man' 'known to the poor girl'[59] – had not been able to forge a sufficient case against McKeeny for Mary Doherty's murder. What they did have was evidence against him for stealing a ewe and a lamb almost two years previously.

In July 1843 – eight months before Mary's murder – a charge of sheep-stealing had been made against McKeeny. A neighbour, Philip Cornish, accused him of stealing a ewe and lamb but the matter was resolved informally, outside of the courts system, and Cornish dropped the charge.[60] The matter was brought to the fore again after Mary's murder as a means of securing a conviction – no matter for what – against McKeeny. Cornish occupied a plot surrounded by the extended McKeeny family: he and his wife would surely have wished to avoid any animosity with the neighbouring extended kin-group. They were, however, now prepared to swear evidence against McKeeny. The fact that a close neighbour was willing to testify against Daniel indicates that he was an outcast from the community after Mary's violent death and that there was a desire to ensure that he did not return to the area. Indeed, Young noted on the day of the murder that 'A great sensation was naturally produced from its being the 1st death of the kind ever committed in this neighbourhood, and everyone (appeared) anxious to discover the murderer'.[61] The strategy of convicting and transporting people for minor offences was a common means at the time of ridding communities of disruptive recidivists, explaining why McKeeny's previous offence of sheep-stealing was revisited following the crown failure to prosecute the case against him for Mary's murder.[62] That said, cases of livestock theft could be treated inconsistently. McKeeny and Gallagher were both transported for sheep and cattle theft – but John Ward (alias John Gallagher), found guilty of stealing a lamb from one John Molloy, received a twelve-month prison term with hard labour on alternate months.[63]

The proceedings at Lifford assizes on 14 March 1845 were reported in detail in the *Londonderry Journal*.[64] The court reporter related how Philip Cornish, his wife Sarah and one John McLaughlin all testified to McKeeny's guilt for sheep-stealing.[65] The Grand Jury must have been left in no doubt as to his character; direct reference was made in the courtroom to the previous charge of murder. The *Londonderry Sentinel* summed up: 'The prisoner was originally apprehended for the dreadful murder of a servant girl, in her master's house, at Culdaff, upon a Sunday last spring, when the family were at chapel; but it was found that the crime could not be brought home to him'.[66] If the case against McKeeny for Mary's murder hinged on circumstantial evidence, the sheep-stealing case does not seem to have been much more conclusive; the key pieces of evidence appear to have been some distinctive black spots on the ears of the ewe and lamb, and a 'tether and swivel' that was attached to the ewe when she was stolen. In sworn evidence, Cornish reportedly stated that a year after the animals disappeared, he saw them grazing on the ground of Samuel Rankin (1803–77), magistrate, of Tirnaleague, Carndonagh, wearing the same tether and swivel.[67] Word reached McKeeny that the Cornishes blamed him for the theft of their animals so he visited Philip Cornish to ask 'what did he and his wife impeach him for'; in response, Sarah called him a 'thief villain'. McKeeny asked whether she had told his mother and promised that if she agreed not do so, 'he would get her another ewe and lamb, though it cost him £5, or that he would pay her whatever sum his brother and James McKeeny would value them at'. The Cornishes later received 15*s*. from McKeeny's father, William. Philip Cornish stated in the dock that he 'did not mention the thing till [the] prisoner was charged with murder, the reason being that he was a stranger in the country; is an Englishman', suggesting that he was merely following the lead of the McKeeny family when they offered to repay him for the lost animals. Sarah Cornish confirmed his evidence 'in all points' and added that on the day following the theft of the animals 'she was in Carndonagh, and there saw the prisoner leading the ewe, the lamb following, and on his perceiving her, he gave the tether a tug and disappeared in the crowd'. Then, in July, she saw the animals (with the distinctive black spots on their ears) at Rankin's, being tended to by a John McLaughlin from Ballagh.[68] The latter also appeared as a witness, and gave sworn evidence that he bought a ewe and lamb at Carndonagh market for 9*s*. from a man that he could not positively identify as McKeeny. He confirmed that there was a piece of tether with a swivel attached to the ewe; that he saw the two animals claimed by the Cornishes at Rankin's; and that the animals had black spots on their ears. A fourth witness was called: Edward Crampsey, who met McKeeny a mile (1.6km) from Carndonagh at 2p.m. on a market day in July 1843, driving a ewe and lamb, a yard-and-a-half of tether attached to the leg of the ewe. He and McKeeny walked to Carndonagh together, and McKeeny told him he was going to sell the animals. The pair met again in the town two to three hours later, when McKeeny told Crampsey that he had sold the ewe and lamb for 9*s*. 6*d*. The final witness was sub-constable John Farmer,[69] who testified that while he 'had [the] prisoner in custody on another charge than this' (that is, the murder) the Cornishes visited the barracks. He stated that McKeeny explained to him after the visit that they 'had a charge against him for a sheep and lamb, but that they had been paid for them'.[70]

Defending McKeeny was Derry-born barrister Thomas Thornton Macklin (b. 1780). The son of a schoolmaster, Macklin was admitted to the Bar in 1805 and unsuccessfully contested the Dublin University seat in parliament in 1807.[71] By 1846 he was living in Buncrana.[72] According to the *Londonderry Journal*, he 'proceeded to address the jury in a very ingenious defence for the prisoner', which was not detailed in the newspaper report. Following this, Chief Justice Doherty addressed the jury, stating that he 'agreed with prisoner's counsel that the case was one of great peculiarity, but left it to the jury to say whether it was so, also one of singular clearness'.[73] It is not known for how long the jury deliberated before arriving at a guilty verdict. Doherty sentenced McKeeny to fifteen years' transportation. Young recorded the verdict in his diary, his vexation palpable:

> At assizes. The murder bills were not found by Gd. Jury, but Donl. McKeeny is found guilty of sheep stealing and sentenced to transportation for 15 years. Another poor fellow sentenced to be hanged, tho' D. McKeeny deserved it much better.[74]

This sitting of the assizes heard two rape cases, a case of the attempted rape of a child by a former police sergeant, and the trial of 20-year-old Michael Doherty for the murder of James Friel at Tullynadall, Fanad, on 27 February. The latter case caused a sensation in the press, with almost verbatim recounting of the questioning and evidence given, but Mary Doherty's murder was mostly only summarized in cursory reports, and her name was not given. The *Waterford Mail* – clearly unaware of the full background to the case – counted McKeeny's trial as among 'some unimportant cases' that were tried in Lifford that day.[75] Horror was expressed in the press reports that issued in the immediate aftermath of Mary's death, enhanced by the fact that Mary was killed in a domestic setting (even if it was also her workplace), violating the 'ideal' of the home for urban, middle-class readers and reporters.[76]

Mary was one of fifteen people murdered across Ireland in March 1844. Eleven were men who died in drunken arguments, sectarian rows or faction fights; the one other female victim had been kicked to death by her husband.[77] In 1844 146 homicides were reported to police, and 129 were tried in the courts (see table 4). The long-held perception of Ireland as more violent than England, Wales or Scotland is borne out in the statistics, with a homicide rate 2.5 times higher than that of England and Wales in the 1850s.[78] Despite her age – reportedly just 14 – not one contemporary source referred to Mary as a child, possibly because of her status as an employed person. In the official records, Mary's killer is still listed as 'unknown', and the verdict: 'Wilful Murder. Robbery appears to have been the object of the offenders, as they took whatever money they could find, and then cut the deceased's throat'.[79]

Table 4. Outcomes of reported homicides tried in the courts in Ireland, 1844

Homicides reported	146
Homicides tried in the courts	129
Convicted, death sentence	19
Convicted, 'o months and under'	1
Declared insane	3
Not guilty on trial	59
No bill found	19
No prosecution	24
Bailed and not tried	4

Source: *Return of outrages … 1842–5* [etc.], pp 1–2.

Occurring before the advent of the telegram, however, only local reporters filed the story, and it was completely forgettable once the regional papers across Britain that syndicated the report moved onto the next scandal. Overall, the geographical remove of this event meant that much of the reporting was superficial, with little understanding of the local socio-economic context. The lack of real interest from even the local court reporter is demonstrated in their careless errors: the *Londonderry Sentinel*, for example, recorded McKeeny's first name as 'Thomas'; and the *Londonderry Journal* reported that McKeeny had lived in Bunagee for 'four or five years', mixing up the accused with the complainant, Philip Cornish, who had moved there from England.[80]

The man sentenced to hanging, referred to by Young, was Michael Doherty of Fanad. The *Londonderry Journal*'s correspondent emphasized Justice Doherty's anguish on delivering the sentence – 'his articulation became indistinct, and he shed tears' – and reported the entreaties of the doomed convict: 'the unfortunate and very guilty young man fell on his knees, and, with hands uplifted and pressed together, implored that he might be transported for twenty years or imprisoned for five years. The witnesses against him, he said, could say what they pleased; but, if wronged by them, he knew "he would not be wronged when he came before the high God of the high Heavens".'[81] The day before his planned execution on 22 April, his sentence was commuted on appeal and, following widespread publicity, to transportation for life.[82]

Whether or not McKeeny killed Mary Doherty, he was fortunate to not have been convicted for murder. W.E. Vaughan's study of murder trials in nineteenth-century Ireland found that in 1844, of nineteen death sentences handed down, only eight were carried out because many of those sentenced to death had their sentences commuted – like Michael Doherty of Fanad. In Vaughan's words, however, 'if there was anything that guaranteed hanging it was committing a murder in the course of committing another felony'. Murder in the course of a robbery was not a common crime – only 5 per cent of murders were committed in those circumstances in the 1830s and 1840s – so it is likely that had McKeeny been found guilty of those crimes, he would have faced the gallows.[83] He was never charged with, or tried for, the theft of 50 shillings from his uncle's house; it can only be presumed that the extended family did not wish that charge to be brought against him, and it is possible that James McKeeny recovered the money privately and informally from his brother, William, or another of Daniel's immediate family. The community in Culdaff could rest easy knowing Daniel McKeeny was never to return, while he joined the ranks of the 160,000 men and women shipped to the Australian colonies in the eighty-year history of penal transportation.[84]

4. To Van Diemen's Land

> a floating dungeon, the prison-home of the exile [...] within its dark and tomb-like bosom were enclosed many suffering spirits, whose crimes had expatriated them from their native land.
>
> Contemporary description of a convict ship lying at Kingstown (Dún Laoghaire) harbour from *Irish Examiner*, 3 September 1845.

McKeeny was transferred – under escort, and probably by cart – from Lifford gaol on 2 May 1845 to Smithfield male convict depot in Dublin, likely in the company of three of his countymen: 14-year-old carpenter Henry Scott, sentenced to seven years for larceny; 19-year-old labourer Bryan McElharr, sentenced to ten years for sheep-stealing; and convicted murderer Michael Doherty, to be transported for life. The four men's names appear in sequence in the depot records and, despite the brevity of their stay, three of the four were recorded as of 'bad' character; only Michael Doherty was 'good'.[1] The depot was located on the eastern side of Smithfield market, near the junction with King Street North. While awaiting transportation, inmates were engaged in making nets and mats for sale and for prison use; picking oakum; carpentry; tailoring of prison suits and clothing for transportees; and shoemaking and knitting for prison use.[2] There was a prison school but, by the admission of state inspectors, the period of incarceration at the depot was so short that 'no observable progress could be expected'.[3] Remaining there for only a few days before his sailing, McKeeny did not have to endure the worst of the conditions that prevailed in Smithfield depot.

Every convict ship was assigned a surgeon-superintendent. Their first interaction with the prisoners was during a pre-embarkation inspection, when he ensured each one was well enough to board ship and complete the journey. Contemporaries complained that both prisoners and prison authorities attempted to conceal cases of chronic illness or disease from the surgeon-superintendent; the prisoners did so to escape the often dreadful conditions in Irish and British prisons, and the authorities to ease congestion and overcrowding, or get rid of particularly troublesome prisoners. For their part, the surgeon-superintendents were keen that all those who embarked would complete the journey alive in order to compensate for the cost of the voyage.[4]

On 7 May McKeeny (and the three prisoners with whom he seems to have travelled from Lifford to Smithfield) embarked for Van Diemen's Land on board the *Ratcliffe*. As the vessel passed out of Kingstown (Dún Laoghaire) harbour, he would have heard the crew on deck giving three cheers – surely a sneer at the miserable prisoners below, convicted of a range of offences and most facing a punishment out of proportion to their crime.[5] Emigration was an accepted fact of life in McKeeny's community, but the majority of those who left would have departed via the more familiar Foyle. If, before going below deck, McKeeny turned to cast his last glance at Ireland – knowing he would never return – he would have seen the low-lying foothills of the Wicklow Mountains instead of the rugged Donegal skyline as the *Ratcliffe* prepared to launch into the grey Irish Sea. From there, the vessel tracked south along the coasts of France, Spain and the African continent before easting to Van Diemen's Land through the southern Indian Ocean along the 39th parallel. The Bay of Biscay could be stormy, and the Cape of Good Hope was known for high westerly winds – the 'roaring forties' – that rushed ships into the buffeting winds and rolling seas to the south of Australia. While conditions could never be pleasant in the hold of a wooden vessel as it tumbled over the oceans for 115 days straight, this sailing of the *Ratcliffe* generated none of the scandal and outrage that other, more fatal voyages did.[6]

Life was highly regulated for the 215 convicts on board, with a daily regimen of work, cleaning and prayer.[7] One report of 1866 related a typical day: convicts were required to be on deck by 6a.m. After breakfast, they were to 'stow away the beds, to sweep, and twice a week to scrub the "between decks", to receive the daily provisions from the third mate (who acted as a sort of purser or steward, under the doctor) and to perform all the duties requisite to keep the portion of the ship occupied by the convicts in a clean and neat condition'.[8] Dinner was served at 12p.m., and supper at 6p.m.

Chores and tasks were allocated to the prisoners according to a rota. This report, published in a ladies' magazine, doubtlessly sanitized the conditions of life during the voyage, but the emphasis on routine and the maintenance of order is indicative of wider patterns in the mid-nineteenth-century convict transportation experience.

The *Ratcliffe*'s surgeon-superintendent, Robert Dobie, was responsible for keeping detailed records of ill-health and ill-repute; he reported that McKeeny had been 'very quiet' during the long voyage. According to his log, the voyage as a whole was relatively uneventful. Just one death occurred – that of a Private John Jennings on 15 July, apparently from an abscess beneath his scalp – and the surgeon noted, 'the prisoners were remarkably healthy throughout' with the exception of one who required hospitalization on arrival in Hobart, the result, Dobie felt, 'of a broken down constitution from hard drinking and exposure to all weathers as a cab driver in Dublin'.[9] Dobie attributed the relative and general good health of the prisoners to the ten tons of potatoes taken aboard in Kingston, which, 'by proper management, a moderate daily supply, lasted till nearly a month beyond the equator'. He also credited 'the benefit of a remarkably dry and roomy ship'.[10] Dobie's cursory summary of the long voyage – just two manuscript pages – glossed over the inescapable truths of personal hygiene, vermin and pests on board, particularly in steerage, and the inevitability of water ingress when waves broke over the vessel. The nosological table appended to Dobie's log records a range of infectious diseases – typical outcomes of unsanitary and overcrowded conditions – among the crew and convicts during the long voyage: 50 cases of catarrh, 13 of diarrhoea, 3 of scrofula, 2 of dysentery and 1 of herpes. McKeeny ('McEaney' in Dobie's sick list) was one of those who suffered from diarrhoea, reporting as unwell from 1 to 7 July.[11]

Nor did Dobie make any mention of the disputes that must have arisen between the 215 men who lived in cramped quarters for almost four months – no verbal abuse or foul language, no petty thefts, no arguments over rations or work, no regional rivalries. In his 1862 account of the prison hulks lying at Woolwich (vessels that remained permanently in dock as floating prisons), Henry Mayhew observed that whatever good was achieved by the prisons was 'effectually destroyed' by the hulks, where a reformed prisoner would be 'thrown amongst brutal companions'.[12] The same diversity of offender and range of ages and life experiences surely existed on the transportation ships.

The *Ratcliffe* landed in Hobart on 30 August 1845.[13] Founded as a penal colony in 1804, the settlement nestled at the foot of Mount Wellington benefited from the fresh water of the Derwent River and the deep harbour, and industries like whaling, shipbuilding and milling thrived. It grew quickly, becoming the administrative capital of Van Diemen's Land from 1812. The 1830s saw significant development, with the building of sandstone churches. McKeeny arrived just three years after the place was officially designated a city; by 1852, it had 24,000 inhabitants and was one of the largest urban centres in Australia.[14] The convicted Young Irelander John Mitchel described arriving in Hobart in 1850: 'Hobart-town has quite an imposing appearance from the water, standing out against its grand mountain background'.[15] The 'pretty villas' of the wealthier settlers were ornamented by 'luxurious gardens'.[16] Convict ships, whaling vessels and small fishing boats thronged the harbour.

McKeeny's life in the penal colony is documented in detail in astonishingly rich official records (fig. 8). This 'paper panopticon' has been identified as 'part of a wider nineteenth-century revolution in personal identification and data collection'.[17] Without photography or fingerprinting, the authorities depended on detailed and stringent descriptive records for convict surveillance. Each prisoner's height, eye and hair colour, visage and distinguishing scars, birthmarks or tattoos were recorded, along with their literacy, living direct family members, and occupation (the latter facts were self-reported). McKeeny's distinguishing marks were unremarkable: a lancet scar on his right arm, freckles, and a missing nail from his right thumb.[18] While these records are impressive and exciting, they cannot be used uncritically; it cannot be assumed that convicts obliged by providing the authorities with absolutely truthful or accurate information; Irish scholars are all-too familiar with the wide margins evident in the self-reporting of respondent's ages in the census, for instance, usually (but not always) the result of innumeracy or lack of knowledge. That said, historian Richard Ward found that 'with at least some convicts unable, or unwilling, to provide the kind of comprehensive, precise and truthful information expected – for the most part convicts appear

NAME, Mc Keeny Donald **No.** **Pn.**

Trade ....
Height (without shoes) ..
Age ....
Complexion .... fresh
Head .... Oval
Hair............... Dk Brn
Whiskers .... None
Visage............. Oval
Forehead .... Small
Eyebrows .... Dk Brn
Eyes .... Grey
Nose .... large
Mouth .... Small
Chin .... Medm
Native Place ....
Remarks............ freckled lancet mark Rt arm lost nail of left thumb

NAME, Mc Elhaw Bryan **No.** **Pn.**

Trade ....
Height (without shoes) .
Age ....
Complexion .... fresh
Head .... Oval
Hair............... Dk Brn
Whiskers .... None
Visage............. Oval
Forehead .... Small
Eyebrows .... Dk Brn
Eyes .... Blue
Nose .... Small
Mouth .... Medm
Chin .... do
Native Place ....
Remarks............ Scar above left Eye - do back of Rt hand -

8. Daniel McKeeny's convict reference file (courtesy of Tasmanian Archives, CON18/1/43, image 190).

to have acquiesced in the face of state authority by providing accurate statements of their age'.[19] The deliberate supply of false or misleading information has been interpreted as a form of resistance, while recent scholarship has emphasized the complexity of these records, which were 'bureaucratic acts that depended [...] not only on the framework set out from above, but also on the capacity and willingness of prison officers on the ground, such as turnkeys, to undertake with rigour these sorts of routine bureaucratic tasks'.[20]

On arrival, male convicts were marched to the prison barracks for processing. Built in 1821, the squat complex of two-storey brown-brick buildings sat just minutes from the docks in the heart of the developing town. The 'paper panopticon' continued to accumulate information: prisoners' occupations were noted, and they were stripped to the waist and any distinguishing marks were recorded to assist with identification in the event of absconding.[21] From the prison barracks, each prisoner was assigned to a penal station.

Van Diemen's Land penal colony was in a unique phase of its history when McKeeny was transported there: the unpopular and ultimately scrapped probation system (1839–53). Replacing the former system whereby convicts worked for free settlers who housed and fed them, or in public works, under probation, each prisoner had to complete a period of 'probationary' government service (i.e., public works) and detention on arrival before proceeding to the private workforce. During probation, convicts would be subject to 'rigorous and uncompromising discipline tempered with moral and religious improvement'.[22] At the time of McKeeny's arrival, the Van Diemen's Land penal colony was struggling to build, staff and manage new stations to provide the 'ganged' accommodation required by the probation system – essentially a massive public-works project.[23] McKeeny's period of probation was initially eighteen months but was increased to twenty-one months, presumably because of his recalcitrance.[24]

He laboured at Salt Water River, Deloraine, Fingal, Launceston, Cascades, Longmarsh Dam, O'Brien's Bridge, Hobart, Tunbridge and Longford stations. Salt Water River and Cascades were located on the Tasman Peninsula in the far south-east of Van Diemen's Land, where the most feared penal stations were clustered. Fingal, in the north-east of the peninsula, operated from 1841 to 1848 when

400 convicts, including McKeeny, laboured to clear lots for sale to establish a new township; similarly, Deloraine station was set up to house convict labourers on road and bridge works.[25] No matter where McKeeny was stationed, the labour assigned to him was indeed 'hard' – the backbreaking work of clearing land for white colonial 'free' settlers and laying roads to encourage and facilitate the extraction of resources and generation of the market economy on indigenous lands. A contemporary described the ecological desecration as settlers 'fight for every acre of land against trees from one to twenty yards in circumference'.[26]

McKeeny continued to be a disruptive force in his new surroundings and protested the deprivation of his liberty through repeated instances of ill-conduct and attempts at escape. His conduct record – tightly written, highly abbreviated and littered with penal officers' signatures – is a litany of offences.[27] On 10 December 1847 he was imprisoned in the prisoners' barracks for three months, with hard labour, for 'not proceeding as directed by a constable'. On 26 September 1848 he was sentenced to twelve months' imprisonment and hard labour in the prisoners' barracks for absconding. On 13 August 1849 he was placed in solitary confinement for six days for 'disobedience of orders'; on 8 December 1849 he was sentenced to six months' imprisonment with hard labour for 'cruelly illtreating one of his master's horses' – a crime that concords with his known previous history of violence. On 1 March 1850 his existing sentence was extended by twelve months for absconding; less than three weeks later, on 19 March, he was placed in solitary confinement for seven days for 'refusing to work'; three weeks later, on 4 April, he had his original sentence extended by a month for 'Misconduct in absenting himself from work on a frivolous plea of illness'. A month later, on 6 May, his existing sentence was extended by another two months for a charge of 'idleness'. At this time (6 May 1850) he was assigned to a chain gang, where he remained for ten months, until 5 March 1851. On 27 July 1850 he received ten days in solitary for 'Misconduct in allowing a fellow prisoner to enter his sleeping berth at night'.[28] McKeeny's sentence was extended by six months on 5 September 1850 for absconding. He then seems to have remained on good behaviour for a time – except for another attempt at absconding in January 1851 – and even had three months of his sentence remitted for good conduct in May 1851. In early 1852 he returned to form, however, receiving one month of hard labour for refusing to work on 9 February 1852, and on 4 March was set to seven months solitary confinement for absconding. On 25 June 1852 his existing sentence was extended by a further three months for 'disobedience of orders and neglect of duty'; on 8 September 1852 he received seven days solitary confinement for being absent without leave; and on 30 October 1852 he was charged with larceny of a sum under £5. He received extensions to his sentence totalling twenty-four months, bringing his sentence to seventeen years and pushing his scheduled release date to autumn 1862.

McKeeny absconded for the sixth and final time on 29 June 1853, disappearing from the sight of the colonial authorities and their 'paper panopticon' for good. Given his conduct record in the penal colony and the repeated extensions to his sentence, it is unsurprising that he should have pursued escape with increasing single-mindedness.

I have not been able to establish with certainty what became of him after June 1853, but there are three possible scenarios. First, that he successfully escaped and lived out his days in a safe location; second, that he died in the course of his escape or shortly afterwards; and third, that he died while under sentence. The second and third options are extremely unlikely. There are no records for him (or any variation of his name) in the extensive archives of the penal colony after 5 July 1853; had he died under sentence, or within the colonies, this almost certainly would appear in his record. And statistically, the average death rate for those serving sentences of more than six years was only 2 per cent; the average rate of male deaths after sentence was slightly lower again.[29]

That leaves the first option: a successful escape. It is tempting to suppose him the same 56-year-old Daniel McKenny (note the variant spelling) recorded in the US census of 1880. America would have been a natural and safe choice of destination, out of reach of the British and colonial authorities. It is unlikely that McKeeny ever returned to Ireland; anyone caught returning after absconding from transportation risked a death sentence.[30] This theory is supported by local folklore, according to which Daniel McKeeny's family moved to America after his conviction.[31] McKeeny had *2s. 6d.* lodged with the convict savings bank in September 1848 – the germination of a fund to support his escape?[32] While it can never be known for sure, it is worth exploring what this path would have looked like for McKeeny.

Like convicted Young Irelander John Mitchel just three months earlier, in April 1853, McKeeny may have managed to reach Sydney (was he in disguise, like Mitchel, who dressed as a priest?), stow away aboard a vessel plying the Pacific crossing to San Francisco – possibly attracted by the wild rumours circulating of California's expansive goldfields[33] – and make his way eastward overland to New York (or, like Mitchel, to sail from San Francisco to Cuba and on to New York via New Orleans).

Both the Daniel who absconded in Van Diemen's Land and the Daniel who appeared in New York in 1880 were of Irish birth and were the same age. Daniel McKenny of Brooklyn declared his profession as 'junk dealer', not an unlikely transition for a former farm labourer finding himself in an urban setting. He was married to Irish-born Catherine, aged 45, and they had six children, all of whom had been born in New York, placing Daniel McKenny there no later than 1865: 15-year-old Mary J. and 14-year-old William H., who both worked in a carpet factory, followed by Kate E. (11), Maggie (7), Daniel (4) and Sarah (2). (It is tempting to seek replication of McKeeny family naming patterns in these children's names but, in reality, these were perfectly common names for children born to Irish parents and cannot suggest any firm conclusions.) The McKennys lived in an almost exclusively Irish neighbourhood known as Vinegar Hill, adjacent to Brooklyn navy yard, thick with overpopulated tenements and teeming with impoverished, unskilled Irish labourers attracted by the low-wage industries that proliferated in the borough. This Daniel McKenny died in Brooklyn in 1889 aged 65, after what was likely a life characterized by hardship.

Fellow Donegal convict Michael Gallagher's story is more complete. Having been sentenced to ten years' transportation on 19 July 1844 for stealing two cows,[34] he departed Kingstown (Dún Laoghaire) harbour aboard the *Elizabeth and Henry* on 15 February 1845 with 199 other convicts and arrived in Hobart on 9 June for detention at Port Esperance.[35] The long delay between his conviction and transportation was not out of the ordinary; prisoners could wait months in Irish gaols for the next available sailing to the penal colonies. The 'paper panopticon' tells us that Gallagher could not read or write and had scars on his right cheek and on his neck.[36] His mother, Mary, was originally from Co. Armagh and he had brothers named Peter, Patrick and Owen, and sisters named Mary, Ellen and Nancy.[37] He conducted himself well during his penal servitude: his conduct record is sparse, with only one instance of 'disobedience' for remaining in 'a house until a late hour' for which he received two months' imprisonment with hard labour and an exclusion order from the Launceston area.[38]

On 26 April 1850 Gallagher's application for free passage for his wife Mary and their sons John (8) and Daniel (6) – who Mary had managed to keep alive through the worst years of the Famine – to join him in Van Diemen's Land was approved.[39] Two years later, on 30 March 1852, he was granted a conditional pardon (usually, the condition was to remain in Australia) before being freed on 12 April 1855, having served his full sentence.[40] The family remained in Australia and Michael returned to work as a labourer. On 21 February 1872 51-year-old Mary died of hepatitis in the district of Franklin, Tasmania. Michael outlived her by almost twenty-seven years; he died of 'senile debility' at the age of 82, on 17 October 1898 in the same district.[41]

McKeeny was in the course of stealing 50*s*. from his uncle when – likely fearful of her eyewitness testimony to his crime – he killed Mary Doherty. What he wanted the money for is anyone's guess, but it is not unreasonable to suggest that he wished to buy passage aboard an emigrant ship. Writing with reference to nineteenth-century Irish female convicts who benefited from assisted migration programmes to North America, historian Elaine Farrell states that 'It is likely that inmates who wished to emigrate both exploited and were grateful for the system that enabled them to do so'.[42] Even convicted murderer Michael Doherty managed – with a mixed conduct record that included an instance of breaking into a woman's apartment bearing a firearm – to secure a conditional pardon in 1856.[43] Looking at the subsequent life stories of Michael Gallagher and Michael Doherty – even if they are only snapshots presented through the eyes and ink of colonial administrators and penal officials – presents an alternative life-course for Daniel McKeeny, had he been able to adapt to life under sentence and await release. His conduct record indicates, however, that the adjustment was impossible for him.

While studying events, lives and the shape of a community in the immediate run-up to the Famine, it is impossible not to wonder how Mary Doherty and Daniel McKeeny would have fared through those years. While Co. Donegal was not the worst affected part of the country, there was a generalized level of suffering and deprivation and those most prone to income precarity (the elderly, people with disabilities, lone mothers and their children) suffered the worst and the earliest. In 1847 Carndonagh workhouse increased its accommodation from 600 to 800, while applying admittance criteria and inmates' rules more stringently to keep the numbers down as the collection of poor rates declined, creating a financial crisis for the institution.[44] The diary of Culdaff landlord George Young indicates the distress experienced in the parish during the Famine. Young first heard of the failure of the potato harvest on 1 September 1846, while he was visiting London; he simply recorded, 'Very bad accounts from home of the Potatoes, and also of the turnips in some places'.[45] By late November, one Sunday was 'appointed for Prayer and Humiliation on account of Potato failure'.[46] In January 1847, he began works in a byre on his property to serve as a soup kitchen; it opened on 13 February, serving sixty gallons of soup.[47] Soon, he was receiving requests for support from those wishing to emigrate; by summer, he had requests from 'a great number of tenants' for money to buy seed oats but confessed to his diary that he 'scarcely gave to any, as I felt convinced many of them were imposing on me'.[48] Meanwhile – labouring long hours each day – McKeeny and his fellow working male convicts were fed 4,500 calories per day, probably well in excess of the diet on which many of his former neighbours in Culdaff subsisted during the Famine.[49]

Conclusion: bloodstains painted over

> The bloody spots are still on the wall of the house and the people had to paint it red to cover the spots. They traced the kiln and got her body very badly burned and the baking spoon in her hand.
>
> Dúchas Schools' Collection. Testimony from Patrick Shiels aged 75, from Muff, Culdaff, 1938.

Mary Doherty's existence would have gone completely unrecorded had she not been murdered. With the exception of this fact, she is completely invisible in the archives of church and state. No census records, or parish birth, death or burial registers survive for the period of her short existence. Her only footprint is that made by her killer. Similarly, Daniel McKeeny and the Gallaghers speak to us through time mainly as people touched by the imperial penal system. When I set out to research and write this book, I had in mind a reconstruction of Mary's life. I wanted to reach my hand across fields and time but found that I was grasping at air. I have attempted to piece together what her short life may have looked like, as well as the lives of those around her and those who invoked her name and the dreadful circumstances of her death to attempt to ameliorate the terrible vistas they themselves faced. This has meant drawing on the full of the historian's toolkit, piecing together scraps of information and laying them against the backdrop of the wider historical contexts of the age, and interpreting the contours and patterns that emerge. In the words of historian Malcolm Gaskill,

> My aim was to scavenge 'a landscape cluttered with the detritus of past living' to see what the reassembled pieces said about what people once saw and felt. This is micro-history, which by drilling deep unearths evidence of human consciousness, both familiar and extraordinary. Past lives are dots in a big picture.[1]

The memory of Mary's violent death survived the humanitarian devastation and abandonment of traditional cultural practices wreaked by the Famine and subsequent mass emigration. These events rapidly accelerated a shift in mentalités that emerged from the 1820s and 1830s, culminating in what Angela Bourke refers to as the jettisoning of 'rich resources in imagination, memory, creativity and communication'[2] – to remain a quiet part of local Culdaff lore for generations. In 1938 75-year-old Patrick Shiels from the nearby townland of Muff told a version of the story to a child attending the parish school (see transcript in Appendix 2). She was participating in the Schools' Collection, a project initiated by the Irish Folklore Commission that involved 5,000 schools and over 50,000 children nationwide to collect local lore and traditions from family and neighbours in 1937–9.[3] Shiels correctly remembered McKeeny's fate as that of 'a sheep thief [...] caught and transported for life'. Mary, however, was transposed from servant to the daughter of a rich family. The story had taken on the tropes of the fireside thriller, embellished through decades of retelling. Along the way, someone added the fabrication that McKeeny attempted to dispose of Mary's lifeless body in a lime kiln two miles (3.2km) away at Laraghirril, near Bocan church, drops of her blood on the road guiding mass-goers to the terrible discovery of the murder scene in Bunagee. In a final flourish, the storyteller related how the family had to keep the kitchen wall painted red because Mary's bloodstains could never be washed away. The motif of the blood that will not wash away is a common one in Ulster folklore; it was said in parts of Ulster that the stain of blood spilled by suicide could never be removed.[4] Similarly, in local Culdaff lore, the theme of enduring stains recurs: one tale of a man killed in an accident with his cart and horse (believed to have been 'a fairy horse') emphasized that 'from that day to this where the man was killed, no grass grew'.[5]

Ghost storytelling (*taibhseoireacht*) had been a popular form of rural entertainment in the nineteenth century, but the 1930s rendering of the story of Mary's murder shifts traditional *taibhseoireacht* into a space tinged by the endemic, systemic misogyny of mid-twentieth-century Ireland.[6]

Today, a small handful of people living in the area recall versions of the story that they heard many years ago from their parents or

9. Extant remains of the McKeeny home.

grandparents. As Terence Dooley wrote in relation to the murder of eight people in an arson attack in Co. Louth in 1816, such events are 'not something to be remembered locally with pride. There were too many raw nerve ends'.[7] My informants are not named here but are identified individually by letters A–F, designated in the order in which I was in contact with them.

Informant A heard the story from his father, who was born around 1925: that a girl was killed during a robbery; that the walls could never be whitewashed afterwards as the bloodstain always came through; that the family who lived in the house went to America after the murder; and that the sound of fiddle-playing can be heard coming from the old homestead if you walk past the site at night. He was the only informant able to correctly identify the exact site on which the murder took place (fig. 9).

Informant C heard the story from his mother: 'I remember my mother telling me about it. Apparently, the girl was left alone in the house and was found murdered on the parents' return. The person suspected was seen washing his hands in a well. The house was supposed to be in the area around Carthage. [...] I took it for granted that everyone heard that story.' This is the only informant who mentioned the murderer washing his hands, a variation on the question of McKeeny scrubbing his hand with sand that was made so much of during the investigation and trial.

Informant D heard the story as a child from a young woman who worked in her family's business: 'I heard something like that too but in Carthage [...] when we were kids and out walking, as us wains were sent out every day usually the baby in the pram, one of the girls who worked in our house [...] from Bocan used to point at a house and tell us a girl was murdered there. Maybe she just made it up to amuse us but might have heard something herself as a child'.

Informant F knew roughly the site of the house where the murder occurred, reiterated the detail about the bloodstained wall and, interestingly, named the family as 'Kane' – only a step away from the name 'McKeeny'. To quote: 'There was an old house near where [named person] now lives. There was supposed to be someone murdered there. I think the people were Kane, there was supposed to be blood on the walls. Never remember anyone living there. We used to rob apples there [*in the*] '60s. Possible late '50s early '60s, don't remember who I heard it from'.

Finally, Informant E had no specific information and did not retell the story but added, 'I heard at the time a Traveller was blamed but they never got him'. Like the other incorrect additions to the story, this reflects particular attitudes prevailing in mid- to late twentieth-century Ireland.

Daniel McKeeny's parents and siblings appear to have left Bunagee after his crime; those he named as his family have left no trace in local burial records or in the civil or church records. The local tradition that they emigrated seems likely. It is worth considering the possibility that they felt unable to remain in the locality.[8] His uncle James and his descendants remained in their home and small farm until the direct family line became extinct and the plot was purchased by a neighbour in 1933. The nearby cluster of McKeeny homes in the heart of Bunagee also gradually transferred to others by sale or inheritance, until the name disappeared from the area in the 1950s.[9]

McKeeny committed at least two crimes in Ireland and had a litany of offences recorded against him in Van Diemen's Land. Were his actions those of a hardened recidivist? Or acts of rebellion against an imperial authority that often imposed excessively harsh sentences on the poorest and most desperate? Either way, the purpose of this book is not to pass judgment on McKeeny. The murder of Mary Doherty provides some insights into the norms of rural life in pre-Famine Ireland: the means by which crimes and disagreements were resolved informally, the justice system's dependence on landlords as paternalistic figures of authority and leadership, and how communities might employ the formal legal system to purge disruptive elements.

I set out to tell Mary's story. The lack of surviving official records at local and national levels limited the possibilities, shifting the focus onto the treatment of her case and tracing the lives of the other principal characters in the story: Daniel McKeeny, Michael Gallagher and Mary Gallagher. If the details of Mary's short life remain out of reach, her presence overshadowed the lives of those three people for the next four decades. Her killing flung McKeeny and the Gallaghers into each other's orbits. She was valued little in life by those whose home she worked in, and little in death by those who instrumentalized her murder in desperate attempts to secure their own futures. The plan hatched by Michael Gallagher and his wife Mary demonstrates the lack of options open to women who were left, for whatever reason, to support a household alone. Rebecca Solnit refers to the non-fiction writer as 'a tracer of the cracks and sometimes a repairwoman, and sometimes a porter or even a vessel for the most precious cargo you can carry, the stories waiting to be told'.[10] I have attempted to usher the 'precious cargo' of these people's stories from past obscurity; to restore voice and agency to Mary Doherty and other people on the margins, whose only trace in the record is of transgressions committed by or against them.

Appendix 1

EXTRACTS FROM THE DIARY OF GEORGE YOUNG OF CULDAFF HOUSE, 1844–5, RELATING TO THE MURDER OF MARY DOHERTY

Spelling, punctuation and capitalization are presented as in the original transcript produced by Amy Isabel Young ('A.I.Y.') in the 1920s. Editorial interpolations are presented in square brackets ([]).

[p. 257] 10th [Mar. 1844] Shortly after church I was informed by Henderson that a murder had been committed near Carthage. We all hurried up after a few minutes, and found Jas. McKeeny's servant girl, Mary Doherty, with her throat cut and much burned, and his son's chest broke open, and robbed of above 50/–. After searching about, Jn. Harvey, and Dr Layard arrived, when we held an Inquest. Billy McKeeny's son Donl. being suspected, and having told me a different account from the true one, of his having gone to Chapel, &c. was arrested in the evening, and remanded till tomorrow. A great sensation was naturally produced from its being the 1st death of the kind ever committed in this neighbourhood, and everyone (appeared) anxious to discover the murderer. Mr Wickham arrived about 6 o'clock, and set off for Derry in pursuit of some suspicious characters.
11th I was busy taking additional evidence about the murder [p. 258] which make the case against D. McKeeny still more suspicious.
13th Jn. Harvey, and Chas. Miller, Mr Rankin, and Mr Wickham again attended, and put off Petty Sessions till tomorrow. We brought Nancy McKeeny's 'Dumby' to show us where Donal McKeeny passed him on Sunday. Mr Tate, Mr Creery's cousin, arrived per Mail Car from Moville on a visit.
14th Philip Cornish called to say he had heard that Jas. Kearney and Moran's son had seen Dl. McKeeny going to Jas. McKeeny's house shortly before the murder. We submitted Dl. McKeeny both on the charge of sheep stealing and murder, and he went off this morning.
17th walked with Mr Tate, Creery, and Williams to Claggan shore.

25th I had Mr Craig engaged in making a sketch of part of Bunagee and Muff, to explain the scene of the late murder at Jas. McKeeny's.
28th J. Harvey, Mr Rankin, and I had another investigation about the murder at Jas. McKeeny's, at the Loan Fund Office. We had all the inhabitants in attendance for half a mile round, and gained some strong additional evidence against Donl. McKeeney.
31st I walked with D.H. as far as Bunagee new road, just before Church time, chiefly to examine more particularly into some points concerning Donl. McKeeny's movements on the day of the murder. Mr Creery performed the evening service for us in the Office.
[...]
[p. 257] May 3rd We had another investigation about Bunagee murder, in consequence of 5/– having been found in Billy McKeeny's turf stack. Mr Foy arrived about Uncle Knox's portrait.
4th Uncle Knox came down and sat for above 2 hours for his portrait in the little room off the Drawing-room. Jn. Harvey sent me a copy of a letter from Donl. McKeeny to his father to look for a sovereign he had hid in the roof of the house. I sent the Police to search for it, but they could not find it.
[...]
[p. 258] 12th [June] Mr Tate (who arrived with Mr Creery on Monday), is marking the places on the map of Bunagee, showing the various tracks taken by Donl. McKeeny on the day of the murder, as proved in the several Informations. [This map was burned in Culdaff House in 1922. A.I.Y.]
[...]
[p. 262] 17th [June] At Assizes. [...]
18th The murder case examined. Creery dined with Gd Jury, and sung.
19th I called on Judge Torrens, and then attended a consultation of the Crown Lawyers, who decided on putting off D. McKeeny's trial till the next Assizes, in hopes of getting further evidence. Tate arrived about 12, and dined with the Grand Jury.
[...]
[p. 262] 16th [August] I had a letter from Mr Tierney, with a copy of Gallagher's information against Dl. McKeeny, as to a confession he made to him in Gaol about the murder.
[...]

[p. 268] 15th March [1845]. At Assizes. The murder bills were not found by Gd. Jury, but Donl. McKeeny is found guilty of Sheep stealing [p. 269] and sentenced to transportation for 15 years. Another poor fellow sentenced to be hanged, tho' D. McKeeny deserved it much better.

Diary of George Young, Culdaff, 1827–75
[typescript copy by Amy Isabel Young].
PRONI D/3045/3/1–2; microfilm MIC586/13.

Appendix 2

THE STORY OF MARY'S MURDER AS TOLD LOCALLY IN 1938

Once there were rich people living in Bunagee and they had a daughter about fifteen years of age. One Sunday the parents went to eleven o'clock Mass and left the child to keep house.

While they were away someone came and asked her for the money. (He was a sheep thief and was caught and transported for life), so she would not give it. When he saw she would not have him get it he lifted a knife off the table and killed her.

Then fearing anyone would get her he carried her away; and when he was going past a lime-kiln in Larahirl which was burning and there he buried her poor body in flames.

When the people were coming home from Mass they saw drops of blood along the road. When they traced them they came to the child's house to find a baking dish with the half-mixed 'doe' for a cake in it and the wall badly spotted with blood and a knife covered with blood to the handle.

The bloody spots are still on the wall of the house and the people had to paint it red to cover the spots. They traced the Kiln and got her body very badly burned and the baking spoon in her hand.

'Treachery' told to Anna Deeny by Patrick Shiels, aged 75, from Muff, Culdaff. The Schools' Collection, vol. 1123, p. 238, available at www.duchas.ie/en/cbes/4493804/4422484.

Appendix 3

DIGITAL SOURCES

The initial research for this project was undertaken throughout Covid-19 lockdowns and while living at a far remove from major archives. Digital resources were invaluable in progressing the project.

Maps

The first-edition (1834) Ordnance Survey sheet covering Culdaff (sheet 5) can be accessed at www.geohive.ie.

The same map series was annotated by valuators working for the valuation in 1855–7; their marked-up copy can be seen at www.askaboutireland.ie, along with *Griffith's valuation* printed lists detailing heads of household and the Annual Rateable Valuation of every plot of land, published in 1857.

Convict Reference Files

The National Archives of Ireland (NAI) holds records relating to the transportation of convicts to Australia, known as Convict Record Files (CRF) and viewable onsite on microform. CRFs, beginning in 1836, contain petitions from thousands of convicts and their dependants. Scans of the NAI microforms are available freely online via Trove (https://trove.nla.gov.au).

Newspapers

Irish Newspaper Archive, available via subscription, allows users to search or browse Irish local and national newspapers from the eighteenth century to the present.

Census records

Irish census records, including household returns, are digitized and freely available via www.census.nationalarchives.ie, with coverage varying by county for the years 1821–91, and full coverage for the years 1911 and 1901. Household returns are not available for Culdaff for the years 1821–51, but data tabulated at local and regional levels provides useful context; reports are freely available at histpop.org. Historic USA census household returns are available via several paid subscription sites.

Registers of births, deaths and marriages

Civil and parish registrations are freely available online at www.irishgenealogy.ie; parish records for Culdaff have also been digitized by the National Library of Ireland (https://registers.nli.ie/parishes/0358), but only from 1838. Locally, nineteenth-century burial records are patchy.

Notes

ABBREVIATIONS

CRF	Convict Reference Files (NAI)
CSO/RP	Registered Papers of the Chief Secretary's Office (NAI)
DIB	*Dictionary of Irish biography*, online edition, available at www.dib.ie
JP	Justice of the Peace
NAI	National Archives of Ireland
NLI	National Library of Ireland
PRO	Public Records Office (London)

INTRODUCTION

1 Mary Gallagher's petition to the lord lieutenant was supported by the parish priest of Templecarn, south Donegal, while her application to join her husband in Van Diemen's Land, granted in 1850, states that her place of residence was 20 miles (32km) away, in Ballyshannon (NAI, CRF 1844 G26). She may have relocated in the intervening years. It was typical for memorials to be signed by local grandees like MPs or members of the clergy (W.E. Vaughan, *Murder trials in Ireland, 1836–1914* (Dublin, 2009), p. 310).

2 Mary Cullen, 'Breadwinners and providers: women in the household economy of labouring families, 1835–6' in Maria Luddy and Cliona Murphy (eds), *Women surviving: studies in Irish women's history in the 19th and 20th centuries* (Dublin, 1990), pp 85–115 at p. 87.

3 NAI, CRF 1844 G26: North West Circuit, County of Donegal, Report by Edward Tierney, 2 and 4 Sept. 1844.

4 Vaughan, *Murder trials in Ireland*, p. 304.

5 John Brewer, 'Microhistory and the histories of everyday life', *Cultural and Social History*, 7:1 (2010), pp 87–109 at p. 91.

6 Ibid.

7 David Fleming, 'Cycles, seasons and the everyday in mid-eighteenth-century provincial Ireland' in Raymond Gillespie and R.F. Foster (eds), *Irish provincial cultures in the long eighteenth century* (Dublin, 2012), pp 133–54 at p. 133.

8 Brian Bonner, *Our Inis Eoghain heritage: the parishes of Culdaff and Cloncha* (Dublin, 1972), p. 223.

9 J.W. Scott, 'Storytelling', *History and Theory*, 50 (2011), pp 203–9 at p. 207.

10 Similarly, Terence Dooley notes that in local Co. Louth and Co. Monaghan lore, the name of one of a group of convicted murderers of 1816 was always remembered, but the names of their victims were never recalled: *The murders at Wildgoose Lodge: agrarian crime and punishment in pre-Famine Ireland* (Dublin, 2007), p. 58.

11 Julia Laite, *The disappearance of Lydia Harvey: a true story of sex, crime and the meaning of justice* (London, 2021), p. ix.

1. LIFE IN CULDAFF IN 1844

1 Ordnance Survey, first-edition, six-inch-to-one-mile (1:10,560); Co. Donegal, Sheet 5; Culdaff, 1834, available at www.virtualtreasury.ie/item/LBC-OS-6-503 (accessed 3 Apr. 2024); *National inventory of architectural heritage*, available at www.buildingsofireland.ie (accessed 1 Mar. 2024). The reference to the 'new Bunagee road' is in Diary of George Young, Culdaff, 1827–75 [typescript copy by Amy Isabel Young], PRONI D/3045/3/1–2; microfilm MIC586/13, 27 Mar. 1841, p. 207.

2 Logainm: bunachar logainmneacha na hÉireann, available at www.logainm.ie (accessed 1 Mar. 2024).

3 Murdoch Mackenzie, *Maritime survey of Ireland* (London, 1776), vol. i, chart 22.
4 *Census* 1841.
5 *National inventory of architectural heritage*, available at www.buildingsofireland.ie (accessed 1 Mar. 2024).
6 Samuel Lewis, *A topographical dictionary of Ireland* (2 vols, London, 1837), vol. i, p. 400; also given in *The parliamentary gazetteer of Ireland ... in 1844–5* (Dublin, 1846), vol. i, p. 550; William Shaw Mason, *A statistical account; or, Parochial survey of Ireland* (3 vols, Dublin, 1814–16), vol. ii, facing p. 174.
7 The diary of George Young refers to salmon boats working the Culdaff River (22 Apr. 1841, p. 209).
8 *Census* 1841; Lewis, *A topographical dictionary*, vol. i, p. 550.
9 Ordnance Survey, first-edition.
10 *National Inventory of Architectural Heritage*.
11 Bernard Burke, *A genealogical and heraldic history of the landed gentry of Ireland* (London, 1912), p. 301.
12 Construction date from *National inventory of architectural heritage*, available at www.buildingsofireland.ie (accessed 1 Mar. 2024). Lewis, *A topographical dictionary*, vol. i, p. 550.
13 Edward Chichester, 'Statistical account of the parish of Cloncha' in Mason, *A statistical account*, vol. ii, pp 176–89 at p. 184.
14 Letter of John Harvey to 2nd Marquis of Donegal, 18 Dec. 1833, NAI, CSO/RP/1833/6202.
15 Death notice of Revd James Knox, *Londonderry Sentinel*, 22 Jan. 1848, transcribed at donegalgenealogy.com (accessed 25 Mar. 2024). Amy Isabel Young, *Three hundred years in Innishowen* ([1929] 2nd ed., Dublin, 2018), p. 203.
16 Lewis, *A topographical dictionary*, vol. i, p. 440.
17 K.T. Hoppen, *Ireland since 1800: conflict and conformity* (2nd ed., Harlow, 1999), pp 38–40.
18 Diary of George Young, 12 Aug. 1841, p. 222.
19 Diary of George Young, passim.
20 *Condition of the poorer classes in Ireland, appendix (e): baronial examination on food [...] etc.* (London, 1835–6), p. 306.
21 Chichester, 'Statistical account of the parish of Culdaff', pp 156–7.
22 Anon., *Notes of a journey in the north of Ireland in the summer of 1827* (London, 1828), p. 40.
23 Anon., *Notes of a journey*, p. 18. 'Unhosed' here means without stockings.
24 See Claudia Kinmonth, 'Communality and privacy in one- or two-roomed homes before 1830' in Conor Lucey (ed.), *House and home in Georgian Ireland: spaces and cultures of domestic life* (Dublin, 2022), pp 125–44.
25 Claudia Kinmonth, *Irish rural interiors in art* (New Haven, 2006), p. 39.
26 National Museum of Ireland Country Life, available at www.duchas.ie/en/cbes/4493767/4418109/4533747 (accessed 3 Apr. 2024).
27 Charles McGlinchey, *An fear deireanach den tsloinneadh*, ed. Patrick Kavanagh, Desmond Kavanagh and Nollaig Mac Congáil (Dublin, 2002), pp 52–3. I refer to the Irish-language edition of this text as it is more faithful to the memoir McGlinchey dictated to Patrick Kavanagh; the English-language version published in 1986 was heavily edited by Brian Friel.
28 Dúchas Schools' Collection, 'Old crafts' from Michael Doherty aged 50, from Ture, Co. Donegal, available at www.duchas.ie/en/cbes/4493767/4418109/4533747 (accessed 3 Apr. 2024).
29 Chichester, 'Statistical account of the parish of Culdaff', p. 156.
30 Francis Lucas Molloy, 'Statistical account of the parish of Clonmany' in Mason, *A statistical account*, vol. i, pp 174–95 at pp 183–4.
31 Molloy, 'Statistical account of the parish of Clonmany', p. 186.
32 Anon., *Notes of a journey*, pp 19–21.
33 McGlinchey, *An fear deireanach den tsloinneadh*, pp 52–3.
34 *Public medical relief: Royal commission for inquiring into the condition of the poorer classes in Ireland: appendix B* (London, 1835), p. 114.
35 'The workhouse' website, available at www.workhouses.org.uk (accessed 3 Apr. 2024).
36 *National inventory of architectural heritage*, available at www.buildingsofireland.ie (accessed 1 Mar. 2024).

37 Chichester, 'Statistical account of the parish of Culdaff', p. 160; Chichester, 'Statistical account of the parish of Cloncha', p. 181.
38 *Parliamentary gazetteer*, vol. i, p. 429; the first part of the quote is from Chichester, 'Statistical account of the parish of Cloncha', p. 181.
39 Chichester, 'Statistical account of the parish of Culdaff', p. 159.
40 N.M. Wolf, *An Irish-speaking island: state, religion, community and the linguistic landscape in Ireland, 1770–1870* (Madison, WI, 2014), p. 3. Margaret Kelleher, *The Maamtrasna murders: language, life and death in nineteenth-century Ireland* (Dublin, 2018) contains excellent analysis on bilingualism and the process of language-shift in nineteenth-century Ireland (pp 28–58).
41 Garret FitzGerald, 'The decline of the Irish language, 1771–1871' in Mary Daly and David Dickson (eds), *The origins of popular literacy in Ireland: language change and development, 1700–1920* (Dublin, 1990), pp 64, 70–1.
42 G.B. Adams, 'The 1851 language census in the north of Ireland', *Ulster Folklife*, 20 (1974), pp 66–8.
43 McGlinchey, *An fear deireanach den tsloinneadh*, p. 55.
44 Molloy, 'Statistical account of the parish of Clonmany', pp 184–5.
45 Chichester, 'Statistical account of the parish of Cloncha', p. 182.
46 McGlinchey, *An fear deireanach den tsloinneadh*, p. 41.
47 Emrys Evans, 'The Gaelic dialect of Urris, Inishowen, Co. Donegal' (PhD, Queen's University Belfast, 1965), pp x–xi, available at https://pureadmin.qub.ac.uk/ws/portalfiles/portal/201388458/Evans_The_Gaelic_62516868.pdf.
48 Katie Barclay, *Men on trial: performing emotion, embodiment and identity in Ireland, 1800–45* (Manchester, 2019), pp 149–55; Kelleher, *The Maamtrasna murders*, pp 90–2, 108–9.
49 Molloy, 'Statistical account of the parish of Clonmany', p. 192.
50 David Fitzpatrick, 'A share of the honeycomb: education, emigration and Irishwomen', *Continuity and Change*, i:2 (1986), pp 217–34 at p. 222.
51 *Census* 1841.
52 Cormac Ó Gráda, 'School attendance and literacy before the Famine: a simple baronial analysis', University College Dublin Centre for Economic Research Working Paper Series (2010), p. 27, available at www.ucd.ie/economics/t4media/WP10_22.pdf (accessed 10 Mar. 2024).
53 Lewis, *A topographical dictionary*, vol. i, p. 400; also given in *Parliamentary gazetteer*, vol. i, p. 550.
54 John Logan, 'The dimensions of gender in nineteenth-century schooling' in Margaret Kelleher and J.H. Murphy (eds), *Gender perspectives in 19th-century Ireland: public and private spheres* (Dublin, 1997), pp 36–49 at pp 36–9.
55 'Conduct registers of male convicts arriving in the period of the probation system', 1 Jan. 1840–31 Dec. 1853, Donald McKeeny, Donegal per *Ratcliffe* (1845), Libraries Tasmania, CON33/1/69, p. 123, available at https://stors.tas.gov.au/CON33–1–69$init=CON33–1–69p123 (accessed 3 Apr. 2024) [hereafter 'Conduct register'].
56 *Minutes of the committee of council on education*, HC 1852–3 (London, 1853), pp 1057–8.
57 Molloy, 'Statistical account of the parish of Clonmany', p. 186.
58 Seán Beattie, 'A Clonmany rector's woes: life in Inishowen in the 1820s', History of Donegal website, available at https://historyofdonegal.com/2017/09/03/a-clonmany-rectors-woes-life-in-inishowen-in-the-1820s/ (accessed 21 Nov. 2023).
59 Frances Browne, *The star of Attéghéi* (London, 1844), p. xi.
60 'Shuífeadh na fir fá an chisteanaigh ag seanchas agus ag inse scéalta agus ag ceoltóireacht. […] Choinneochadh cuid acu an toigh ag gabháil go ham luí le greannaireacht. Ní raibh aon dadaí eile le déanamh ag na fir in éis an clapsholas'. McGlinchey, *An fear deireanach den tsloinneadh*, p. 55.
61 Honoria Galwey, *Old Irish croonauns* (New York, 1910).
62 Diary of George Young, 30 Mar. 1841, p. 207; 8 Oct. 1841, pp 226–7.
63 Samuel Carter Hall and Anna Maria Hall, *Ireland: its scenery, character &c.* (3 vols, London, 1841–3), vol. 3, p. 237.

64 Hugh Dorian, *The outer edge of Ulster: a memoir of social life in nineteenth-century Donegal*, ed. Breandán Mac Suibhne and David Dickson (Dublin, 2000), editors' introduction, p. 5.

65 Chichester, 'Statistical account of the parish of Cloncha', p. 188. For context on illegal distilling, I am indebted to David Dickson's essay 'Derry's backyard: the barony of Inishowen, 1600–1850' in William Nolan, Liam Ronayne and Mairead Dunlevy (eds), *Donegal, history and society: interdisciplinary essays on the history of an Irish county* (Dublin, 1995), pp 422–3.

66 Chichester, 'Statistical account of the parish of Culdaff', p. 153.

67 *Tenth report of the commissioners of inquiry into the collection and management of the revenue arising in Ireland, Scotland &c.*, HC 1824 (446) (London, 1824), p. 313.

68 *Condition of the poorer classes in Ireland, appendix (e): baronial examination on food [...] etc.* (London, 1835–6), p. 306.

69 *Condition of the poorer classes*, p. 306; *Tenth report*, p. 313.

70 Dickson, 'Derry's backyard', p. 435.

71 Diary of George Young, 16 Apr. 1841, p. 208.

72 Ordnance Survey, first-edition.

73 Anon., *Notes of a journey in the north of Ireland*, pp 14–15.

74 Richard McMahon, *Homicide in pre-Famine and Famine Ireland* (Liverpool, 2013), p. 23.

2. A DREADFUL CRIME

1 They could have attended either the older chapel around at Aughaclay (Templemoyle) or the imposing new parish church at Bocan; the former was slightly closer via an old path across the fields, but the latter is more likely given that more contemporaneous burials from Bunagee are found at Bocan, including members of the extended McKeeny family.

2 Vaughan, *Murder trials in Ireland*, p. 35.

3 Young, *Three hundred years*, p. 205.

4 See Kevin McKenna, 'Elites, ritual and the legitimation of power on an Irish landed estate, 1855–90' in Ciaran O'Neill (ed.), *Irish elites in the nineteenth century* (Dublin, 2013), pp 68–82.

5 Richard McMahon, 'The court of petty sessions and society in pre-Famine Galway' in Raymond Gillespie (ed.), *The remaking of modern Ireland* (Dublin, 2004), pp 101–37 at pp 122–5.

6 Oliver McDonagh, *Ireland: the Union and its aftermath* (Dublin, 2003), p. 170.

7 McMahon, 'The court of petty sessions and society in pre-Famine Galway', p. 122.

8 Quoted in 'Appalling murder in Ennishowen', *Nenagh Guardian*, 23 Mar. 1844.

9 'Atrocious murder and robbery', *Freeman's Journal*, 15 Mar. 1844; 'Appalling murder', *The Era*, 24 Mar. 1844.

10 No census records survive for Co. Donegal for 1821–51; nor do any parish records survive that might have recorded baptismal or burial details for Mary Doherty or her killer.

11 *Griffith's (primary) valuation*, searchable on the Ask About Ireland website, available at www.askaboutireland.ie/griffith-valuation/ (accessed 1 Mar. 2024) [hereafter *Griffith's valuation*].

12 Dickson, 'Derry's backyard', p. 433.

13 Patrick Fitzgerald and Brian Lambkin, *Migration in Irish history, 1607–2007* (Houndmills, 2008), p. 162.

14 See Fitzgerald and Lambkin, *Migration in Irish history*, pp 158–64.

15 Diary of George Young, 2 Apr. 1841, p. 207.

16 Diary of George Young, 4 Feb. 1843, p. 247; 'Ship news', *The Times* (London), 13 Feb. 1843.

17 C.J. Houston and W.J. Smyth, *Irish emigration and Canadian settlement: patterns, links and letters* (Toronto and Buffalo, NY, 1990), pp 15–16.

18 NAI, CRF 1844 G26: Copy of statement made to Board of Superintendence of Lifford Gaol, 5 Aug. 1844.

19 Quoted in Cullen, 'Breadwinners and providers', p. 106.

20 General Register Office, death certificate of James McKenney [*sic*], 11 Jan. 1866.

21 Quoted in Cullen, 'Breadwinners and providers', p. 104.

22 Chichester, 'Statistical account of the parish of Culdaff', p. 160.

23 Harriet Martineau, *Letters from Ireland* (London, 1852), p. 65.

24 Cullen, 'Breadwinners and providers', pp 99–100, 105.

25 McGlinchey, *An fear deireanach den tsloinneadh*, pp 43, 55.

26 'State of the thermometer, at Belfast, in the shade' [for the dates 5–7 Mar. 1844], *Belfast Newsletter*, 8 Mar. 1844.

27 Descriptive lists of male convicts, 1828–53, *Ratcliffe*, 29 Aug. 1845, Libraries Tasmania, CON18/1/43, available at https://libraries.tas.gov.au/family-history/convicts-in-van-diemens-land-now-tasmania/convict-life/convict-records/what-is-online/#articleBody (accessed 1 Mar. 2024). It is possible that the lancet mark was from smallpox inoculation. I have not found evidence of a scheme in Culdaff parish but an inoculation programme was undertaken in neighbouring Clonmany parish by Molloy in the early nineteenth century; he wrote that while it was the 'only distemper that affect[ed] the population […] the people here, with few exceptions, are prejudiced against it, thinking that the vaccine system will protect them from the ravages of the small-pox only three years' (Molloy, 'Statistical account of the parish of Clonmany', p. 184). Chichester reported that in Culdaff parish, 'vaccination [is] superstitiously resisted' (Chichester, 'Statistical account of the parish of Culdaff', p. 157).

28 McKeeny's family members are listed alongside his sentence and crime in 'Indents of male convicts', 1824–53, Libraries Tasmania, CON14/1/20, p. 299, available at https://libraries.tas.gov.au/family-history/convicts-in-van-diemens-land-now-tasmania/convict-life/convict-records/what-is-online/#articleBody (accessed 1 Mar. 2024).

29 Tithe Applotment Books, 1823–37, NAI: parish of Culdaff, townland of Carthage (1828), pp 39–41, available at http://titheapplotmentbooks.nationalarchives.ie (accessed 1 Mar. 2024).

30 Information on the Cornish family is from the General Register Office (marriage and death certificates) and *Griffith's valuation*. Mary Cornish is also listed as recipient of a loan from Culdaff Loan Fund on 7 July 1860 (Account book of the Culdaff Loan Society, Co. Donegal, Mar.–July 1860, NLI, MS 23,063, line 366).

31 *Griffith's valuation*.

32 Ordnance Survey, first-edition; a key to 'Conventional signs and writing used on the 1:2500 plans of the Ordnance Survey' is available at https://maps.nls.uk/os/characteristic-sheets/ (accessed 9 Mar. 2024).

33 Kevin Danaher, *Ireland's vernacular architecture* (Dublin, 1975), pp 12, 17.

34 K.T. Hoppen defines the lower end of a 'substantial' farm as between 10 and 20 acres; I employ his alternative term, 'family farmers' here as applicable to those in possession of a mean of 20 acres (*Ireland since 1800*, pp 40–1).

35 Information on the various branches of the McKeeny family is from the General Register Office, birth, death and marriage certificates; and Catholic Parish registers for Culdaff, NLI Microfilm 05466/02, available at https://registers.nli.ie/parishes/0358 (accessed 1 Mar. 2024). I have made exhaustive searches, but gaps remain in the McKeeny genealogy.

36 Chichester, 'Statistical account of the parish of Culdaff', p. 160.

3. BRINGING HOME THE GUILT

1 The proliferation of the surname Henderson has hindered attempts to identify this officer.

2 Jim Herlihy, *The Irish Revenue Police: a short history and genealogical guide to the 'poteen hussars'* (Dublin, 2018), p. 36.

3 Herlihy, *The Irish Revenue Police*, pp 220–1, 238.

4 *Constabulary (Ireland): report from the select committee of the House of Lords*, HC 1854, 53 (London, 1854), p. 6.

5 Herlihy, *The Irish Revenue Police*, pp 29, 161, 227.

6 Ibid., p. 47.

7 Ibid., p. 50.

8 Ibid., pp 67, 69.

9 Brian Griffin, 'The *Irish police*, 1836–1914: a social history' (PhD, Loyola University Chicago, 1991), p. 67, available at https://ecommons.luc.edu/luc_diss/3028/ (accessed 28 Mar. 2024).

10 Jim Herlihy, *The Royal Irish Constabulary: a short history and genealogical guide* (Dublin, 1997), pp 75, 120.
11 Griffin, 'The Irish police', pp 808–10, 867.
12 Diary of George Young, 11 Mar. 1844, pp 257–8.
13 Ibid., 13, 14 Mar. 1844, p. 258.
14 Ibid., 25, 28 Mar. 1844, p. 258. Emphasis in original.
15 Ibid., 31 Mar. 1844, p. 258.
16 Ibid., 3 May 1844, p. 257.
17 Ibid., 4 May 1844, p. 257.
18 Ibid., 12 June 1844, p. 258. This map was lost in the burning of Culdaff House in 1922.
19 'Horrible murder in Ennishowen', *Belfast Newsletter*, 22 Mar. 1844.
20 Diary of George Young, 10 Mar. 1844, p. 257.
21 *Parliamentary gazetteer*, p. 429.
22 'Horrible murder in Ennishowen', *Londonderry Journal*, 19 Mar. 1844; Diary of George Young, 14 Mar. 1844, p. 258.
23 *Slater's commercial directory of Ireland* (Manchester, 1846).
24 Evidence given by Revd E.M. Clarke in *Report from the select committee of the House of Lords appointed to consider the state of the lunatic poor in Ireland*, HC 1843, 193 (London, 1843), p. vii.
25 Information from Lifford Old Courthouse and Gaol website, https://liffordoldcourthouse.com/history/ (accessed 27 Feb. 2024).
26 Turnkeys' reports, 1829–31, Donegal County Archives P/26/1 (1), 7, 8 July 1829; references to Irish being spoken are at 22, 26 Dec. 1829, 7 Jan. 1830. Digitized at www.donegalcoco.ie/culture/archives/digitised%20archives/selected%20digitised%20archives/#d.en.21867 (accessed 6 Apr. 2024).
27 Turnkeys' reports, 24 Aug. 1829, is one example of many.
28 Turnkeys' reports, 9, 11 Aug. 1829, 5, 11 Feb. 1830.
29 *Londonderry Journal*, 23 July 1844. These works were carried out and in 1847 prison inspectors reported favourably on the new solitary cells and on the new chapel, built in 1846–7 (*Twenty-sixth report on general state of prisons of Ireland*, HC 1847–8, vol. xxxiv, 253 (London, 1848), p. 53).
30 Turnkeys' reports, 23, 27 Aug., 29 Sept., 27 Dec. 1829.
31 Lewis, *A topographical dictionary*, vol. i, p. 260.
32 Vaughan, *Murder trials in Ireland*, p. 86. See Breandán Mac Suibhne's description of Lifford, its courthouse and gaol in *The end of outrage: post-Famine adjustment in rural Ireland* (Oxford, 2017), pp 153–5.
33 Diary of George Young, 17, 18 July 1844, p. 262; Bridget Hourican, 'Hill, Lord George' in *DIB*.
34 Quoted in Vaughan, *Murder trials in Ireland*, p. 90.
35 Kelleher, *The Maamtrasna murders*, p. 69.
36 'Judge Perrin', *Londonderry Journal*, 23 July 1844.
37 'Crown Court', *Londonderry Journal*, 23 July 1844.
38 Ibid.
39 'The trials', *Ballyshannon Herald*, 26 July 1844.
40 Diary of George Young, 19 July 1844, p. 262.
41 Kelleher, *The Maamtrasna murders*, p. 103.
42 'The trials', *Ballyshannon Herald*, 26 July 1844.
43 Death notice of Francis Flood, *Londonderry Sentinel*, 26 Aug. 1859; *Griffith's valuation*, Parish of Killymard, p. 81.
44 'Crown Court', *Londonderry Journal*, 23 July 1844.
45 NAI, CRF 1844 G26.
46 NAI, CRF 1844 G26: Petition of Michael Gallagher to lord lieutenant, 5 Aug. 1844.
47 Information about Clarke is from *Londonderry Sentinel*, 21 Apr. 1863.
48 NAI, CRF 1844 G26: E.M. Clarke, 15 Aug. 1844 (copy).
49 Diary of George Young, 16 Aug. 1844, p. 262.
50 NAI, CRF 1844 G26: George Young, 17 Aug. 1844.
51 NAI, CRF 1844 G26: Joseph Johnson and B. Geale Humfrey, 5 Aug. 1844; and Queries and answers by George Young.
52 NAI, CRF 1844 G26: George Young, 17 Aug. 1844.
53 NAI, CRF 1844 G26: Queries and answers by George Young. Young's copy of the letter does not appear to have survived. Young's diary (4 May

1844, p. 257) noted 'a letter from Donl. McKeeny to his father to look for a sovereign he had hid in the roof of the house' – not to his brother.

54 NAI, CRF 1844 G26: North West Circuit, County of Donegal, Report by Edward Tierney, 2 and 4 Sept. 1844.

55 NAI, CRF 1844 G26: Copy of letter by Judge Robert Torrens, 10 Aug. 1844.

56 Quoted in Vaughan, *Murder trials in Ireland*, p. 290.

57 *Gentleman's Magazine*, vol. xlv, May 1856, pp 523–4.

58 All information on Doherty is from Patrick M. Geoghegan, 'Doherty, John' in *DIB*.

59 'Murder and robbery', *Ballyshannon Herald*, 15 Mar. 1844.

60 'Horrible murder in Ennishowen', *Belfast Newsletter*, 22 Mar. 1844.

61 Diary of George Young, 10 Mar. 1844, p. 257.

62 Joan Kavanagh provided this interpretation of transportation sentencing in correspondence.

63 *Londonderry Journal*, 23 July 1844.

64 'Crown Court. Friday, March 14', *Londonderry Journal*, 18 Mar. 1845.

65 The third witness may be the John McLoughlin listed as living at plot 26 in Carthage, further up the mountain, in 1856 (*Griffith's valuation*, parish of Culdaff, p. 51).

66 'Sheep stealing', *Londonderry Sentinel*, 22 Mar. 1845.

67 Rankin's information is from General Register Office, death certificate; and *National inventory of architectural heritage*, www.buildingsofireland.ie (accessed 6 Apr. 2024).

68 This person has not been identified. The surname McLaughlin is extremely common in Inishowen. Several McLoughlin/McLaughlin families are listed in Ballagh in *Griffith's valuation*, but no head-of-household named John McLaughlin. Ballagh is just north of Malin village, 11km from Bunagee.

69 I have not been able to match this name to a serving constabulary officer in Culdaff in 1845. Two John Farmers are recorded in Jim Herlihy's guides but, judging by their service numbers, neither of these had joined by 1844–5. It is possible that the newspaper reported the wrong name: Herlihy, *The Royal Irish Constabulary: a short history and genealogical guide*, p. 232; idem, *The Royal Irish Constabulary: a complete alphabetical list of officers and men, 1816–1922* (Dublin, 1999), pp xviii, xx.

70 The details in this paragraph are as reported in 'Crown Court. Friday, March 14'. *Londonderry Journal*, 18 Mar. 1845.

71 *King's Inns admission papers, 1607–1867*, ed. Edward Keane, P. Beryl Phair and Thomas U. Sadleir (Dublin, 1982), p. x; 'Dublin University Borough', History of Parliament online, available at www.historyofparliamentonline.org/volume/1790–1820/constituencies/dublin-university (accessed 6 Apr. 2024).

72 *Slater's directory*.

73 'Crown Court. Friday, March 14', *Londonderry Journal*, 18 Mar. 1845.

74 Diary of George Young, 15 Mar. 1845, pp 268–9.

75 'Assizes intelligence', *Waterford Mail*, 26 Mar. 1845.

76 Mary Hatfield, *Growing up in nineteenth-century Ireland* (Oxford, 2019), pp 87–93.

77 *Returns of outrages reported to the Irish Constabulary Office, Dublin Castle, during the month of March 1844* (Dublin, 1844).

78 S.J. Connolly, 'Unnatural death in the four nations: contrasts and comparisons' in idem (ed.), *Kingdoms united? Great Britain and Ireland since 1500* (Dublin, 1998), pp 200–14 at p. 206.

79 *Returns of outrages … March 1844*.

80 'Sheep stealing – the Culdaff murder', *Londonderry Sentinel*, 27 July 1844; 'Crown Court. Friday, March 14', *Londonderry Journal*, 18 Mar. 1845.

81 'The Fannet murder', *Londonderry Journal*, 18 Mar. 1845.

82 NAI, TR 5, P 40. Incidentally, Doherty was transported aboard the *Ratcliffe*, the same vessel as McKeeny (CRF 1845 D 10; CRF 1845 misc16). His transportation records stated that he was a 'very quiet' man ('Conduct register', CON33/1/69, p. 38).

83 Vaughan, *Murder trials in Ireland*, pp 320, 323, 377, 389.

84 Katherine Foxhall, 'From convicts to colonists: the health of prisoners and the

voyage to Australia, 1823–53', *Journal of Imperial and Commonwealth History*, vol. 39, no. 1 (2011), pp 1–171 at p. 3.

4. TO VAN DIEMEN'S LAND

1 Smithfield male convict depot transportation register, NAI, GPO TR 5, lines 1299–1302.

2 *Twenty-sixth report on general state of prisons of Ireland*, HC 1847–8, vol. xxxiv, 253 (London, 1848), p. 18.

3 Ibid., p. 19.

4 Foxhall, 'From convicts to colonists', p. 3.

5 As described by an eyewitness to the departure in *Freeman's Journal*, 19 May 1845.

6 For example, in 1849 several Dublin teenage girls were found to have been sexually abused during their voyage to Sydney as part of the so-called 'Earl Grey' orphans' scheme; another girl, Dolly Newman, died of haemorrhage during the voyage, likely due to miscarriage: Philip Harling, 'Assisted emigration and the moral dilemmas of the Victorian state', *The Historical Journal*, 59:4 (2016), pp 1027–49.

7 Number of convicts aboard given in 'Reports of ships arrivals with lists of passengers. Tasmania', 2 Apr. 1844–18 Sept. 1846, Libraries Tasmania, MB-39-1-8, available at https://stors.tas.gov.au/MB2-39-1-8 (accessed 13 Apr. 2024).

8 'Life aboard a female convict ship', *The Englishwoman's domestic magazine*, vol. i (1866), pp 311–17 at p. 313.

9 Robert Dobie, Journal of His Majesty's hired convict ship *Ratcliffe*, 7 Apr.–4 Sept. 1845, PRO, Admiralty Records, Records of Medical and Prisoner of War Departments, ADM 101/63: convict ships, available at Trove, https://nla.gov.au/nla.obj-1599521487/view (accessed 13 Apr. 2024).

10 Dobie, Journal.

11 Ibid.

12 Henry Mayhew and John Binny, *The criminal prisons of London and scenes of prison life* (London, 1862), p. 202.

13 'Conduct register', CON33/1/69, p. 123.

14 Peter Bolger, *Hobart town* (Canberra, 1973).

15 John Mitchel, *Jail journal* (New York, 1854), p. 239.

16 Mitchel, *Jail journal*, p. 261.

17 Richard Ward, 'State authority and convict agency in the paper panopticon: the recording of convict ages in nineteenth-century England and Australia', *Australian Historical Studies*, 52:4 (2021), pp 509–32 at p. 509, DOI: 10.1080/1031461X.2020.1858896.

18 'Conduct register', CON33/1/69, p. 123.

19 Ward, 'State authority and convict agency', p. 511.

20 Donald Fyson and François Fenchel, 'Prison registers, their possibilities and their pitfalls: the case of local prisons in nineteenth-century Quebec', *The History of the Family*, 20:2, The family and the history of the prison (2015), pp 159–307 at p. 184.

21 Helen Rogers, '"A very fair statement of his past life": transported convicts, former lives and previous offences', *Open Library of Humanities* (2015), DOI: http://dx.doi.org/10.16995/olh.27.

22 Richard Tuffin and Martin Gibbs, '"Uninformed and impractical"? The convict probation system and its impact upon the landscape of 1840s Van Diemen's Land', *History Australia*, 17:1 (Mar. 2020), pp 1–217 at pp 92–3.

23 Tuffin and Gibbs, '"Uninformed and impractical"?', pp 94, 97.

24 Appropriation lists of convicts, 1845–6, Libraries Tasmania, CON27/1/11, available at https://librariestas.ent.sirsidynix.net.au/client/en_AU/tas/search/detailnonmodal/ent:$002f$002fARCHIVES_DIGITISED$002f0$002fARCHIVES_DIG_DIX:CON27–1–11/one; and Convict muster roll, 1845–6, Libraries Tasmania, CON28/1/2.

25 Tuffin and Gibbs, '"Uninformed and impractical"?', p. 102.

26 Johnson Dean, *A trip to California in 1850–3* (Hobart, 1905), quoted in Kay Walsh and J.W. Hooton, *Australian autobiographical narratives* (2 vols, Canberra, 1993), vol. 2, p. 65.

27 All of the information in this paragraph is from 'Conduct register', CON33/1/69, p. 123. The conduct record is supplemented by reports from *Hobart Town Gazette*, 26 Sept. 1848, 26 Feb., 3 Sept. 1850, 14 Jan. 1851, 5 July 1853,

available at https://libraries.tas.gov.au/Digital/TGG (accessed 13 Apr. 2024).

28 Same-sex relations were not uncommon in the penal colonies: see Catie Gilchrist, 'Male convict sexuality in the penal colonies of Australia, 1820–1850' (PhD, University of Sydney, 2004).

29 Janet McCalman and Rebecca Kippen, 'The life-course demography of convict transportation to Van Diemen's Land', *History of the Family*, 25:3 (June–Aug. 2020), pp 345–526 at p. 444.

30 Vaughan, *Murder trials in Ireland*, p. 307.

31 Informant A.

32 'Journal of moneys paid into the savings bank on behalf of convicts', 1838–53, Libraries Tasmania, CON73/1/1, p. 398, available at https://libraries.tas.gov.au/Record/Archives/CON73/1/1 (accessed 13 Apr. 2024). McKeeny's name is rendered 'Donald 'McKennard' in this source.

33 Dean, *A trip to California*, quoted in Walsh and Hooton, *Australian autobiographical narratives*, vol. 2, p. 65.

34 'The trials', *Ballyshannon Herald*, 26 July 1844.

35 'Conduct registers', CON33/1/65, p. 79.

36 Ibid.

37 'Indents of male convicts', CON14/1/20, p. 199.

38 'Conduct register', CON33/1/69, p. 79.

39 Ibid.

40 Ibid.

41 Ibid.; 'Indents of male convicts', CON14/1/20, pp 198, 199; death certificates for District of Franklin, Tasmania.

42 Elaine Farrell, '"The salvation of them": emigration to North America from the nineteenth-century Irish women's convict prison', *Women's History Review*, vol. 25, no. 4: *Connecting women's histories: the local and the global* (Aug. 2016), pp 493–695 at p. 628.

43 'Conduct register', CON33/1/69.

44 Hilary McLaughlin-Stonham, *The consequences will be fearful: the Great Famine in County Donegal* (Donegal, 2023), pp 27–9.

45 Diary of George Young, 1 Sept. 1846, p. 281.

46 Ibid., 20 Nov. 1846, p. 283.

47 Ibid., 16 Jan. 1847, p. 285; 13 Feb. 1847, p. 286.

48 Ibid., 27 Feb. 1847, p. 286.

49 McCalman and Kippen, 'The life-course demography', p. 435.

CONCLUSION: BLOODSTAINS PAINTED OVER

1 Malcolm Gaskill, *The ruin of all witches: life and death in the New World* (London, 2022), p. 234.

2 Angela Bourke, 'The baby and the bathwater' in Tadhg Foley and Seán Ryder (eds), *Ideology and Ireland in the nineteenth century* (Dublin, 1998), pp 79–92. See also Seán Connolly, 'Popular culture' in S.J. Connolly, R.A. Houston and R.J. Morris (eds), *Conflict, identity and economic development: Ireland and Scotland, 1600–1939* (Preston, 1995), pp 103–13.

3 Dúchas Schools' Collection, Story from Patrick Shiels aged 75, from Muff, Culdaff, available at www.duchas.ie/en/cbes/4493804/4422484 (accessed 27 Feb. 2024).

4 Thanks to Georgina Laragy for this information.

5 Dúchas Schools' Collection, Story from Fanny McLaughlin aged about 48 years, from Culdaff, available at www.duchas.ie/en/cbes/4493804/4422379 (accessed 27 Feb. 2024).

6 Later local retellings of the murder of Conell Boyle in the Rosses were also found to contain inaccuracies: see Frank Sweeney, *The murder of Conell Boyle, Donegal, 1898* (Dublin, 2002), p. 48.

7 Dooley, *The murders at Wildgoose Lodge*, p. 57.

8 In *The end of outrage*, historian Breandán Mac Suibhne considers the potential impact of his research on the living descendants of those he studies (pp 16–19).

9 Land transfer information is drawn from the Valuation Office cancel books for Carthage, Inishowen, and augmented with information from the Irish civil registers (General Register Office). Any descendants of the McKeeny family are welcome to contact the author for more detailed information.

10 Rebecca Solnit, *Recollections of my non-existence* (London, 2020), p. 239.

Index